W. H. Bartlett

Jerusalem revisited

W. H. Bartlett

Jerusalem revisited

ISBN/EAN: 9783743365278

Manufactured in Europe, USA, Canada, Australia, Japa

Cover: Foto ©ninafisch / pixelio.de

Manufactured and distributed by brebook publishing software (www.brebook.com)

W. H. Bartlett

Jerusalem revisited

JERUSALEM
REVISITED
BY
W. H. BARTLETT.

JEWISH HOSPITAL.

THOMAS NELSON & SONS; LONDON, EDINBURGH & NEW YORK

JERUSALEM REVISITED.

BY

W. H. Bartlett,

AUTHOR OF "WALKS ABOUT JERUSALEM."

LONDON:
T. NELSON AND SONS, PATERNOSTER ROW;
EDINBURGH; AND NEW YORK.

MDCCCLXIII.

Contents.

PAGE

PREFACE ii

CHAPTER I.

From London to Jerusalem.

CRITICAL ASPECT OF EASTERN QUESTION—FÊTE OF THE PLAGUE—INCREASED COMMERCE—ENGLISH FLEET LEAVES MALTA—ALEXANDRIA NEW LINES OF STEAMERS—THE INDIAN MAIL—RACE OF THE STEAMERS—ABOUKIR —LANDING AT JAFFA—RUMOURS OF WARS—ARRIVAL AT JERUSALEM 1

CHAPTER II.

Mount Zion and the English Church.

APPROACH TO JERUSALEM—UPPER AND LOWER POOLS OF GIHON—JAFFA GATE—CITADEL—IMPROVEMENTS—INNS—TOWER OF HIPPICUS—ENGLISH CHURCH—ITS ORIGIN—LONDON SOCIETY FOR PROMOTING CHRISTIANITY AMONG THE JEWS—FOUNDATION—APPOINTMENT OF A BISHOP—HIS ENTRY—COMPLETION OF CHURCH—RESULTS OF MISSION—SKETCH OF PRESENT STATE OF THE CITY, BY MRS. FINN—DIOCESAN SCHOOL—INDUSTRIAL PLANTATION—JEWISH HOSPITAL—EVANGELICAL HOSPICE—CHURCH MISSIONARY SOCIETY—VISIT TO ARMENIAN CONVENT—NEW PALACE, ETC.—CLERICAL SEMINARY—WALK ABOUT MOUNT ZION—CŒNACULUM—TOMB OF DAVID—CHRISTIAN CEMETERIES—ENGLISH BURIAL GROUND—VIEW FROM BROW OF ZION OVER TO THE TEMPLE—THE BRIDGE—WILLIAMS' PRETENDED CORRECTION, ETC.—THE JEWS IN JERUSALEM—THEIR QUARTER—CONDITION, ETC.—JEWISH DISPENSARY 17

CHAPTER III.

Interior of the City, Streets, &c.

STREET OF DAVID—DR. ROBINSON'S TYROPEON—BAZAARS—BAB-ES-SALSALA—VIEW FROM WITHIN—STREET OF THE VALLEY—THE BATH "HAMMAM SHEFA"—ARCHWAYS AND FOUNTAIN—THE TEKEEYEH—STREET OF THE PATRIARCH—HOTELS AND CONVENTS OF THE LATINS AND GREEKS—WEST PORCH OF THE CHURCH OF THE HOLY SEPULCHRE—CHURCH OF SEPULCHRE—HOSPITAL OF ST. JOHN—VIA DOLOROSA—CHURCH OF ST. ANNE—POOL OF BETHESDA (SO CALLED)—INTERIOR OF THE HARAM . . . 84

CHAPTER IV.

The Mount of Olives and the Valley of Jehoshaphat.

TOWER ON THE MOUNT—CHURCH OF THE ASCENSION—ANCIENT TRADITIONS—PANORAMIC VIEW OF JERUSALEM—GARDEN OF GETHSEMANE ALTERED—TRADITIONS—TOMB OF ABSALOM—POOL OF THE VIRGIN—ISAIAH'S TREE—EN ROGEL—ROCK TOMBS OF ACELDAMA 114

CHAPTER V.

The Haram Enclosure.

DIFFICULTY OF ENTRANCE—MR. TIPPING—ADVENTURE OF A FRIEND—MY OWN—RAMBLE ROUND THE EXTERIOR—PRINCIPAL OBJECTS WITHIN—VAULTS—THEORIES OF ROBINSON, WILLIAMS, AND FERGUSSON EXAMINED—PAPER BY MR. S. SHARPE 140

CHAPTER VI.

Matters Miscellaneous.

TOPOGRAPHY OF ANCIENT CITY—WALK ROUND THE WALLS—JEREMIAH'S CAVE—DAMASCUS GATE—ANCIENT CHAMBERS—NORTH-WEST CORNER—EXCURSION TO THE CONVENT OF THE CROSS—STATE OF FEELING IN JERUSALEM—JEALOUSIES AND REPORTS—ROAD TO JAFFA BY BETH-HORON AND LYDDA 178

Preface.

THIS work originated in the general indulgence extended to the Author's first production,[1] the "WALKS ABOUT JERUSALEM." Comparatively inexperienced as he then was in literary composition, and not sufficiently aware of the strong and peculiar interest attaching to the subject in public estimation, he was content to limit that work to the illustration of the more popular objects of investigation, while many other matters of sacred or historical interest were altogether omitted. But the patronage so generously extended to the book, notwithstanding its many imperfections, of course rendered the Author more desirous of supplying its deficiencies.

With this object in view, he succeeded in making an arrangement with his present Publishers, to revisit the Holy City. His first wish was to re-write the former work entirely, incorporating fresh matter and engravings, so as to render it a more complete and satisfactory guide.

[1] Published in 1844.

But upon further consideration, it was thought more desirable to produce a new book, which, while it did not trench upon ground already gone over in his preceding work, might chiefly introduce such subjects as were then either omitted, or but partially illustrated.

But other views concurred in inspiring the writer with a wish to revisit the scene of his labours. In the first place, much has been since written on the subject, and many novel and curious theories put forth, which rendered him desirous of going over the ground again with a fresh eye. Secondly, since the establishment of the Anglican Bishopric, much improvement, it was said, had taken place in the condition of the city. New schools, hospitals, and other institutions had been founded, not only by the Protestants, but the other religious bodies. The place had received a great impulse for improvement, and further and important changes were anticipated. To obtain, as well as communicate, some idea of this new state of things, also contributed to render a second visit desirable.

This statement will serve to show that the present work is not, indeed, what was originally intended, but chiefly of a supplementary character—giving principally new views and descriptions of places slightly, if at all, noticed in the original volume. For correct information as to the progress of improvement and the march of events, the Author must express his great acknowledgments to J. FINN, Esq., F.S.A., H.B.M. Consul in Jerusalem, and his accomplished lady, whose long residence must give the stamp of authenticity to the communications with which they have favoured him. He is besides greatly indebted to Dr. Barclay for many valuable notices; while his old and kind friend, Mr. F. Catherwood,[1] has laid him under fresh obligations, by the loan of several sketches of places either pulled down, or at present inaccessible to research.

W. H. B.

DURING the brief interval which has elapsed between the preparation of this Work and the usual period of publication, the melancholy tidings have reached England of the sudden and premature decease of the Author. Cut off in the flower of his age, and in the full vigour of intellect, after a few hours' illness, he has found a sepulchre in the waters of the Mediterranean, whose shores he had so often, and so successfully, illustrated. It is generally known that his later years were mainly devoted to the production of a series of Pictorial Works, combining the peculiar talents of the author and the artist, and which have been received (it is now gratefully acknowledged) with uniform favour by the public and the press. It was, indeed, no slight encouragement to my lamented brother,

---

[1] By a most painful coincidence this deeply-valued friend of Mr. Bartlett, the companion of his former eastern journeys, has also found (it is believed) an ocean grave. He was in the ill-fated "Arctic" steamer at the time of its loss, and is supposed to have perished, with the greater number of the passengers.

amid the many toilsome and not unfrequently perilous journeys incidental to his literary labours, to find that his efforts were so readily and kindly appreciated, nor does the recollection of this circumstance fail to afford an equal solace to his bereaved family and friends.

With regard to the present Work, I have only to state that it has been deprived of the correcting hand of the Author, who, had he been permitted to return to his native land, and to superintend its passage through the press, would doubtless have removed some blemishes, and given it a form more worthy the approval of its readers. As it is, the distressing circumstance of his decease will be remembered in extenuation of any errors or omissions, which the care of others may possibly have overlooked. It is almost needless to add, that the Holy City, its past history, its present condition, and its future prospects, were to the writer of these pages subjects of peculiar and engrossing interest; and it now affords a melancholy satisfaction to his friends, that he was enabled to revisit Jerusalem, in order to resume a popular narrative, of which the former part was so favourably received by the public.

F. A. BARTLETT.

Newchurch Rectory,
  November 14*th*, 1854.

Engravings on Steel.

		Engraved by	To face Page
1.	MOUNT ZION.—JAFFA GATE, (*Frontispiece*)	E. Brandard.	
2.	JEWISH HOSPITAL, (*Title-page*) ...	C. Cousen.	
3.	PANORAMA, ...	E. Brandard, ...	1
4.	ENGLISH CHURCH AND CONSULATE, AND TOWER OF HIPPICUS, ...	E. Brandard, ...	19
5.	ENGLISH BURIAL-GROUND, ...	C. Cousen, ...	67
6.	VIEW FROM BROW OF MOUNT ZION,	A. Willmore, ...	72
7.	ARCHED STREET AND FOUNTAIN, ...	C. Cousen,	84
8.	WEST DOOR—CHURCH OF HOLY SEPULCHRE, ...	A. Willmore, ...	91
9.	CHAPEL OF HELENA AND CAVE OF THE CROSS,	E. Challis, ...	100
10.	GATE OF THE HOSPITALLER'S PALACE,	E. Challis, ...	102
11.	VIA DOLOROSA,	C. Cousen, ...	108
12.	POOL OF BETHESDA, ...	A. Willmore, ...	112
13.	TELESCOPIC PEEP AT THE HARAM, ...	E. Brandard, ...	124
14.	VALLEY OF JEHOSHAPHAT,	A. Willmore, ...	130
15.	POOL OF THE VIRGIN, ...	C. Cousen, ...	131
16.	ISAIAH'S TREE, ...	C. Cousen, ...	133
17.	EN ROGEL, ...	E. Brandard, ...	134
18.	ACELDAMA, AND TOMBS IN THE VALLEY OF HINNOM,	A. Willmore, ...	135
19.	PULPIT ON THE PLATFORM OF THE HARAM,	E. Challis, ...	153
20.	DAMASCUS GATE, ...	A. Willmore, ...	187
21.	ANCIENT JEWISH CHAMBER, DAMASCUS GATE, ...	E. Challis, ...	188
22.	CONVENT OF THE CROSS, ...	C. Cousen, ...	190

Woodcuts.

	Page
Bay of Aboukir,	9
Jaffa, ...	12
Convent of St. James, Jerusalem,	64
Mount Zion, ...	66
Ancient Sarcophagus, ...	86
Church of St. Anne, ...	111
Specimen of Arabesque, ...	125
Tombs of the Prophets—Plan, ...	129
Interior of Tombs, ...	130
Tombs of the Judges, ...	138
Plan of Tombs, ...	139
Masonry of the Haram, ...	149
Mosque of Omar, ...	153
Plan of Hill of Moriah, ...	167
Plans of Temple, ...	169
Plan of Temple of Karnak, ...	170
Plan of Temple of Jerusalem, ...	173
Gate of Damascus, ...	186

CHAPTER I.

From London to Jerusalem.

CRITICAL ASPECT OF EASTERN QUESTION—FÊTE OF THE PLAGUE—INCREASED COMMERCE—ENGLISH FLEET LEAVES MALTA—ALEXANDRIA NEW LINES OF STEAMERS—THE INDIAN MAIL—RACE OF THE STEAMERS—ABOUKIR—LANDING AT JAFFA—RUMOURS OF WARS—ARRIVAL AT JERUSALEM.

On the 10th of June, 1853, I turned my face a second time towards the walls of Jerusalem, uncertain whether war might not be on the very point of breaking out. Russia was just endeavouring to take another footstep on the road to Constantinople, the ultimate object of her traditionary policy,—at one time astute and undermining—at others, insolent and daringly aggressive, as intrigue or violence might best subserve her object. The contemptible quarrel about the "Holy Places," so warmly disputed by the Greek and Latin monks with their fists and candlesticks at Jerusalem, served as the pretext of fresh demands, which in the nineteenth century threatened to kindle a general conflagration throughout civilized Europe. To the ignorant fanatical hordes of Russia, an object of political intrigue was made to assume the appearance of a New Crusade,—by which the Mussulmans were to be driven into Asia, Constantinople conquered, and the banners of the Greek Church and the Czar planted upon the walls of the Holy City.

It was desirable to strike the final blow before the efforts made for some years past to inspire new life into the decrepit body of Turkey might haply become successful, or before the Greeks, whose wealth and influence was rapidly increasing, should perhaps establish another Byzantine empire; thus robbing the Vulture of the North of the prey he has for so long been watching to seize. The opportunity for a movement had arrived. The temporary dissolution of the "*entente cordiale*" between England and France, consequent on the elevation of Napoleon III., the mutual jealousy and clashing interests of those powers in the Mediterranean, would, it was hoped, prevent them from acting together promptly and decidedly to oppose it. But even should they do so, and the general reprobation of Europe compel the Autocrat to renounce his purpose, still the efforts at resistance made by Turkey would no less ultimately serve his plans. Her internal resources would be consumed for the support of an enormous army; while that fanaticism, which has been the chief obstacle to her improvement, being awakened by so unfair an aggression, would either precipitate the Sultan upon open hostilities, or, if he refused, imperil his very throne. Such were, at least, the anticipations at that time entertained; how signally they have been falsified by the course of events is notorious to every one.

The fate of Jerusalem is necessarily involved with Constantinople; for should the capital—the only part of the Turkish empire displaying any political vitality—fall into the hands of Russia, the whole machine of government is at once subverted, and the provinces of Egypt and Syria would find another master. It was felt, therefore, everywhere, that the present was a most critical moment in the affairs of the East, and no one could foresee the issue of those hostilities into which the aggression of Russia seemed bent on forcing the world.

I repaired to Marseilles, and took passage for Syria in the French government steamer "Osiris." The evening before we left the city occurred one of the most striking processions ever witnessed, especially when its object is taken into account. It was a commemoration of the day on which the last fearful visitation of the plague terminated—a visitation deeply engraved in the memory of the Marseillais. It occurred about a century ago, and cut off a large portion of the population. A picture in the town records the scenes of horror then witnessed, reminding us of those so vividly described by Defoe. The day, like all in this southern clime, was resplendently brilliant; the ships in the harbour were decorated with streamers; the principal shops were closed, and the whole population devoted to enjoyment, and the religious observances of the festival. There is something contagious in the cheerfulness of one of these southern *festas*, in which all classes alike pause from their labours, and appear thoroughly to enjoy themselves, without that riot and turbulence so common in an English holiday. As evening drew near, the booming of cannon over the city indicated that the procession was about to commence. The balconies along the line were decorated with carpets or festoons of bright coloured drapery, and filled with gaily dressed spectators; while those in the streets were either seated in chairs let out for the occasion, or ranged quietly along the causeway, without any of that crushing so indispensable to the enjoyment of a London mob, even when consisting of well dressed ladies and gentlemen. From the window of the hotel, near the corner of the Canebiere, I enjoyed a perfect view of the procession. It opened as usual with a number of priests bearing crucifixes and banners, often very beautifully decorated. After these came a long line of young gentlemen, smartly dressed in white trowsers and blue coats. But the most pleasing and graceful feature was the next,—an immense number of beautiful young girls, dressed in white muslin, and with their hair enwreathed with chaplets of roses, sustaining silken banners inwrought with pictures of the Virgin relieving sufferers in the plague, and other appropriate subjects. Next followed a long double file of women, dressed in grey as penitents; their eyes alone were visible through the opening of their hoods, and they carried candles in their hands. This lengthened procession, which must have numbered many thousands, chanting low and solemn hymns as they filed slowly past on both sides of the road, had something inexpressibly striking, associated as it could not fail to be with the terrible incidents of the plague. An immense number of male penitents, similarly habited, kept up the endless succession, intermingled at intervals with parties of ecclesiastics singing and bearing crosses. By this time it had become quite dark, and the candles carried by the penitents were lighted, and, with numerous splendid silver lamps, borne by the chanting priests, gleamed through the streets with a singularly impressive effect. The heavy tread of a long file of soldiers, and the spirit-stirring strains of military music, contrasting with the sacred and solemn harmonies of the penitents and priests, which had previously been heard, brought to a close the most affecting procession it had ever been my chance to witness.

In glancing round the port of Marseilles, there was abundant evidence that its commercial steam marine had within a few years greatly progressed, though not with the gigantic strides of London or Liverpool. Besides the vessels of the "Messageries Nationales," and other lines trading to Italy and the Levant, there were other companies to Algeria, Corsica, and Spain; and a new line had lately been started to the coasts of Morocco—a country looked upon with covetous eyes by the possessors of Algiers, and which, according to some of the journals, they will ere long be compelled, in self-defence, to conquer and annex. It was matter of pride, however, to see that our countrymen maintained their preeminence; for the finest boat, by common consent, then in the harbour, was the "Euxine," belonging to the Peninsular and Oriental Company, destined in a few days to carry out the Indian Mail to Malta. This has since been thrown into the shade by the superior speed of the "Vectis" and "Valetta."

It was a moment of intense anxiety to the Marseillais; another "crisis" in the interminable Eastern question—for ever recurring and for ever deferred. The French fleet had already sailed from Toulon for the Turkish waters; and the absorbing anxiety was now to know whether England would act cordially with France in resisting the aggression of Russia—an alliance which, from the tone of the journals, seemed ardently to be desired. The "Caradoc," with the second English admiral in command, was then in the harbour, awaiting every hour the arrival of the courier bearing the decision of government. To the mercantile interest of Marseilles, so intimately connected with the Levant, the question of peace or war was one of vital importance; and the state of indecision was grievously complained of as paralysing enterprise, and introducing uncertainty into every commercial operation.

We left Marseilles before the government messenger had arrived, in the "Osiris," French government steamer, for Alexandria direct, and in less than three days anchored in the quarantine harbour at Malta. As we had a few hours to spare I went on shore, where the same excitement prevailed as to the expected sailing of the fleet. From the Upper Barracca the whole squadron was to be seen in all its grandeur, ready to depart at an hour's notice. When the smoke of our steamer appeared in the distance it was supposed to be that of the "Caradoc," which arrived in fact shortly after we left; and that very evening the fleet sailed for Besika Bay: and who could tell what gallant actions — before it returned to its moorings—it might add to the long catalogue of Britain's naval glories!

The display of men of war in the harbour of Alexandria was

far less imposing than in the time of Mehemet Ali; some of those built by him being already almost dismantled. There was still however a respectable force for a power like Egypt; and this was being prepared with as much despatch as the dilatoriness of Oriental habits would permit, in order to assist the Sultan in the anticipated war with Russia. To hasten on the work, many of the labourers had been withdrawn from the new railway to Cairo. Several of these vessels afterwards perished in the disastrous affair of Sinope.

On the other hand, the number of merchant vessels, and more especially of steamers, seemed to have greatly increased. Besides the boats of the Austrian Lloyds, the French "Messageries Nationales," and the "Peninsular and Oriental Steam Navigation Company," forming a little fleet of themselves, there were several screws intended for trading along the coasts of Syria, Asia Minor, and Greece. The growing commerce and importance of these countries is shown in nothing better than this—that three lines of coasting steamers, touching at all the principal ports, are already established, and a fourth is now in contemplation. Even with the absurd restrictions of the quarantine, which prevent passengers leaving Alexandria for the Syrian coast, these vessels are found to pay handsomely; and when free intercourse is established, as it doubtless ere long will be, there can be no doubt that the traffic will prove extremely lucrative. A few years ago not a Lough steamer was to be found in this part of the East. The great affair that keeps everything at Alexandria on the *qui vive* is the arrival and departure of the Indian Mail. So important has this become that the three companies above mentioned, Austrian, French, and English, keep up an eager competition for the conveyance of passengers; and these are so numerous that all the boats are usually well filled. The French were formerly behind the others, their boats being of several years' date, and though very strongly built, not able to keep pace with their rivals;

nor did they pick up more than a few of the passengers. The Austrians had established a very fast line, of which the "Calcutta" had run to Trieste in about 112 hours, thus offering by far the shortest sea passage to those who preferred travelling by land. These boats were small, but of great steam power, and were generally very well filled. The Peninsular Company had lately made great efforts to surpass their rivals, having sent out the "Bengal," a new screw steamer of immense size, which had accomplished the quickest passage ever known from Southampton to Alexandria.

These vessels were now anxiously awaiting the arrival of the mail, already delayed several days beyond its time. At length its landing at Suez was telegraphed, and in a few hours the passengers might be expected. It was now quite a relief in our imprisonment on board to watch the movements in the harbour, and to speculate on which of the ships would get her passengers on board first, and take the lead in the race homewards. Towards afternoon the funnels of the three steamers began to pour forth volumes of smoke, and boats were seen pushing off from the shore with crowds of Indian passengers, who were speedily transferred on board their respective ships, the major part preferring the "Bengal" and "Calcutta," the former of which vessels had already excited great admiration on board the French steamer, not only for her great size, but the singular beauty of her proportions. The evening was lovely, the sky and sea invested with true Mediterranean lustre. At five o'clock, the hour named for departure, the race was evidently about to begin. The "Bengal" took the lead; and the ease with which a vessel of such immense length glided from her moorings, her splendid appearance as she got under way, and the bursts of music simultaneously arising from her decks, created a perfect *furore* among the Frenchmen, who crowded up to the forecastle to witness the spectacle. "Le plus beau bâtiment que j'ai vu de ma vie," enthusiastically exclaimed little Monsieur Blot, our spirited first-lieutenant. And now the French packet followed; but though a handsome vessel, evidently toiled in vain after her magnificent rival, which left her far in the rear. Last of the three, the Austrian boat, the "Calcutta," by far the smallest vessel, started off with extraordinary speed. She rapidly caught up the French boat and left her far behind, straining every nerve to overtake her colossal English antagonist, which, as the contrary wind did not permit the latter to take advantage of her immense spread of sail, there seemed some probability of her doing. The "Bengal," however, continued to take the lead till entirely out of sight, closely followed by the "Calcutta," while the poor Frenchman was left "nowhere in the race." The Company of the "Messageries Nationales," however, determined not to give up their share of the sport, have already ordered some boats of much greater steam power; and, when the railroad to Marseilles shall be completed, will no doubt be formidable rivals to the English and Austrian companies.

On the morning following the departure of the Indian mail, the steamer from Syria arrived. We were transhipped on board of her in the course of the day, and next morning, at an early hour, were steaming out of the harbour for Jaffa. Our course lay for some distance along the coast, which was low and sandy, here and there relieved with a few groves of palm. We soon approached the memorable Bay of Aboukir, with the story of which every child in England is familiar. A chart of the coast lay on the table, and enabled me to understand the formation of the bay, which, owing to the lowness of the shores, could not well be made out from the deck of the vessel. Like the scenes of so many other great events, there was nothing at all striking in the theatre of this terrible sea-fight. The only landmarks on shore are a Turkish castle on a low hill, and another fort upon the shore. The mouth of the bay is marked by a sterile island, from which a ridge or reef of broken rocks extends as far as the fort, forming a shelter from the westerly winds. Beyond is seen the curve of the bay, lined with palm-groves, around which were anchored the ships of Admiral Brueys, on that day so fatal for France, when Nelson, after a long and weary chase, at length came in sight of his enemy.

To my own mind the involuntary rising of national pride, which could not but be awakened at such a spot, was almost lost in the feeling of solemn awe at passing over the graves of so many gallant men, who had there met in mortal conflict. It was singular, too, to be on board a vessel of the conquered nation,— the only countryman of the conquerors. As we approached, the captain, with great courtesy, simply pointed out "Aboukir!" but made no further observation; a feeling of delicacy prevented me from entering upon the subject, and we ran by the spot almost in silence.

Soon after passing Aboukir, the pale colour of the water showed that we were off the mouth of the Nile. The castle and palm-groves of Rosetta were the next objects that broke the monotony of the low and sandy coast. Damietta, so famous in the Crusades, was left at a greater distance. Ranges of abruptly formed sand-hills reflected the rays of the setting sun, as we bore off from the Egyptian coast, and steered directly for that of Palestine. Next morning the line of coast was dimly visible, the hills of Palestine gradually became more distinct, and about three in the afternoon we came to an anchor abreast of Jaffa.

The landing at this place is notoriously difficult, owing to the heavy swell which breaks upon the coast, and the narrow access to the harbour, which is formed by a reef of broken rocks. In bad weather it is often impracticable, so that the steamer is obliged to pass without touching. A story is told of a missionary bound for Jerusalem, who had embarked at Alexandria with the intention of landing at Jaffa; but owing to the bad weather, was carried past to Beyrout. On arriving there the return steamer was about to sail, and rather than perform a land journey of several days, he preferred to take his passage for Jaffa, thinking it very unlikely that he should be a second time prevented from landing. However, on arriving, the weather was so bad that it was impossible to communicate with the shore, so that the unfortunate missionary was carried back to Alexandria. Here he could not land, because he would have been placed in quarantine, and thus was a second time wafted back to Jaffa, when happily the elements were this time propitious, and he was enabled to get on shore.

As soon as the boat was lowered the doctor and commissioner went on shore to obtain *pratique*. We watched their bark as it entered the perilous pass through the rocks, where it seemed completely lost among the breakers, but at length emerged and reached the landing in safety. It was a very nervous piece of business, and my French companion said we were going to pass "un mauvais quart d'heure." Several barks were seen dashing off from the shore, manned by the natives, who, like the boatmen at Madras, have acquired extraordinary dexterity in working through the dangerous swell, which at times completely hid them from view. Into one of these, after taking leave of the courteous captain, we descended amidst much vociferation, and were speedily plunging through the surf, which burst upon the rock-reef. It seemed impossible to escape destruction; but the skilful Arabs struck with a loud shout and pull of their oars through an opening so narrow that there was hardly room for the boat, and we were at once in still water.

A few strokes more brought us up to the landing-place, where the scene of uproar beggars all description. After attaining a precarious footing, we were nearly pushed back again into the watery element by the belligerent Arabs, each seeking to get hold of part of our luggage. It was with great difficulty we could force our way through the water-gate which leads into the town. Here we fell in with the janissaries of the French and English consuls, who conducted us to their respective masters.

Few travellers who have visited Jaffa within the last twenty years can fail to remember the eccentric Signor Damiani, with his dirty pelisse, and his greasy cocked hat, and mock-heroic dignity of deportment. This personage has ceased to officiate as British consul, and has been replaced by Dr. Asaad el Kayat, a native Syrian, who studied the art of medicine in England, and perfectly understands the language. To his abode I was now conducted by his dragoman. Turning up a dirty lane, and ascending a broken stair, we entered the house, which is roughly yet solidly built in the Arabian style: the principal room was furnished with an eye to English comfort; and, after twelve days' confinement on board, it was a luxury to loll upon ample divans, which stood firm on their legs, and inhale the fresh sea breeze, looking out upon the picturesque old port, the subject of classical and sacred tradition, where Noah is said to have launched his ark, and where Perseus delivered the fair Andromeda, chained, doubtless, to one of the wave-worn fragments of rock through which we had just passed. The house almost impended over the sea wall, which was pierced for a gun or two, commanding the mouth of the port; where the swell broke so heavily, that the spray almost mounted to the window. The steamer lay at anchor just off the port, and a few primitive

small craft with lateen sails added to the picturesqueness of
the scene.

There being still no decent inn at Jaffa, the worthy consul
insisted upon our remaining at his house until the following
morning; and this hospitality I found from an album on the
table he was in the habit of extending to our countrymen in
general. Several of his Syrian friends looked in after sunset,
and much anxiety was expressed to know whether the fleet had
sailed. Some persons were seriously alarmed at the prospect of
war, anticipating a general rising of the Moslem population, and
a massacre of the Christians, as soon as news arrived that the
Russians had crossed the Turkish frontier. In general, reports
of all sorts are prodigiously exaggerated in these countries;
partly from their isolation and want of regular newspapers,
and partly from the superstitious fancies and excitable tempera-
ment of the Orientals. At this distance from Constantinople, and
where political details are scarcely understood—the ignorance and
fanaticism of the Turks make but little distinction between their
enemies, the Russians, and their allies, the French and English;
for all these are in their eyes unbelievers, and regarded with hereditary antipathy. The Moslems cannot but be conscious that their
day of power is gone by, and they witness with bitterness the

growing influence of the Franks. They feel that their sway over these fair countries is drawing to its close; and there is a floating tradition among them, that the present year (1853) is destined to behold its downfal. But they are determined not to fall without a struggle: and this feeling is inflamed by the fanaticism of the dervishes, which seems to put forth all its energy for a last expiring effort. Whenever war breaks out, the position of the Christians would, it was feared, become dreadfully insecure; and every packet was awaited with intense anxiety; while, in default of authentic news, all sorts of rumours were in circulation. Although accustomed to make allowance for Oriental exaggerations, I could not but feel that there was much to cause uneasiness, if not alarm, in the threatening aspect of the political horizon.

We left Jaffa early on the following morning; and though not above nine o'clock, the heat was getting insupportable when we dismounted at the only gate of the convent at Ramla, which, like most others in Palestine, is surrounded by a high and strong wall. Leaving our horses in an outer court, we entered the corridor of the convent. Truly, it was a delicious shelter from the burning rays of the sun. The floor was of stone; the walls and arched roof whitewashed, and adorned with frescoes of incidents in the life of its patron saint, Joseph of Arimathea. On two sides the cloister was supported by pillars, and opened into a small garden, overshadowed by a palm-tree and a huge spreading vine, through which the sun could only penetrate in a few places, casting scattered gleams of light upon the cool moist earth below. It was a luxury to sit upon the stone bench in the shade, and fall asleep, lulled by the gentle rustle of the vine-leaves and palm-trees, and hushed by the deep tranquillity of the spot.

There are but three or four Spanish monks in this extensive building, but they keep it in the nicest order. One of these, a venerable man, came forward and gave us the right hand of fellowship. Formerly this convent was a halting-place for all comers; but since the establishment of the English Mission at Jerusalem, the monks are said to look coldly upon the heretics, and sometimes even to deny them admittance. My French companion, however, being a good Catholic, cast the mantle of his orthodoxy over me, and we experienced a warm reception from the brethren. Our first intention was merely to have halted for an hour or two, but the Superior would not hear of this. So fearful was his account of the number of people killed by *coup de soleil*, in consequence of braving the noonday sun, that we were easily persuaded to dine and take our siesta at the convent, and defer our journey to Jerusalem until the heat of the day had subsided.

Although it was four o'clock in the afternoon when we left the convent at Ramla, our journey across the plain was still exceedingly oppressive. At dusk we entered the defiles of the hills, by a road of indescribable ruggedness; and, fairly wearied out, were glad to repose for an hour or two at the village called "Abinjosh," from its being the head-quarters of that turbulent mountain chief. Long before daylight we were again in the saddle, sliding and stumbling over the execrable mountain paths, one series of slippery rocks and stones; and as the stars faded, and the eastern sky began to be tinged with pale rose colour, we fell in with parties of peasants, wending their way, like ourselves, to the Holy City. From the level of the plain at Ramla, we had gradually clambered up to a high table-land, nearly two thousand feet above the sea, everywhere rocky and uneven, strewed with endless stones, and serried with tremendous ravines, whose jagged ribs projected from their sides, giving to the whole district a gaunt, desolate, skeleton-like sort of appearance.

Nothing can be more flat and unimposing than the first view of Jerusalem by the Jaffa road. We passed across a high bleak tract of country, the surface of which is everywhere so

rocky and uneven, that the horse stumbles at every step.
The hills are totally without character, and the general scene
tame, wearisome, and depressing. Here and there, indeed, the
rugged slopes are thinly veiled by terraces of grey olives, or a
poor looking field of corn seems struggling for life in the arid
plain; but the general aspect is sterility itself. In vain do we
seek for any indications of that grandeur of situation and magnificence of architecture indelibly associated with our conceptions
of a city depicted in such glowing terms by the Hebrew poets;
and grievous is the disappointment as a dull line of walls, without any prominent object to relieve their monotony, is pointed
out as that Jerusalem of which the imagination had formed
so different an idea. As we draw nearer, however, the view
becomes somewhat more imposing. The Valley of Hinnom
slopes down on the right, gradually sinking till it forms a deep
and rugged glen beneath Mount Zion, the walls and towers of
which stand out in striking relief. The towers of the citadel
have also an imposing effect, increased by its bold outwork and
profound fosse; while the Jaffa or Bethlehem gate, of handsome
Saracenic architecture, forms an admirable centre to the picture.
The line of walls is here, in all probability, nearly if not quite
identical with that of the first or original wall of Zion, the most
ancient of the three by which Jerusalem was defended, although
no part that meets the eye appears older than the time of the
Saracens. These battlemented bulwarks, flanked with towers,
perforated with openings for arrows, and overlapped by a lofty
minaret, have a strikingly picturesque effect. Moreover, as this is
the principal entrance to the city, it presents, in the morning and
evening, a very animated spectacle. Women, bearing baskets of
grapes, figs, or pigeons from the neighbouring villages; peasants,
driving before them asses laden with vegetables; Bedouins, conducting files of camels, bearing masses of stone for new buildings,
continue to pour along in a continuous stream. Monks slowly
amble in upon their asses from some of the neighbouring con-

vents, or European residents dash past from their country houses or summer encampments in the neighbourhood. Large flocks of black-haired goats, from which the city is supplied with milk, ascend from the Valley of Hinnom. And at this hour there is a show of life and animation which might seem to indicate an important and flourishing city.

CHAPTER II.

Mount Zion and the English Church.

APPROACH TO JERUSALEM—UPPER AND LOWER POOLS OF GIHON—JAFFA GATE—CITADEL—IMPROVEMENTS—INNS—TOWER OF HIPPICUS—ENGLISH CHURCH—ITS ORIGIN—LONDON SOCIETY FOR PROMOTING CHRISTIANITY AMONG THE JEWS—FOUNDATION—APPOINTMENT OF A BISHOP—HIS ENTRY—COMPLETION OF CHURCH—RESULTS OF MISSION—SKETCH OF PRESENT STATE OF THE CITY, BY MRS. FINN — DIOCESAN SCHOOL — INDUSTRIAL PLANTATION — JEWISH HOSPITAL—EVANGELICAL HOSPICE—CHURCH MISSIONARY SOCIETY—VISIT TO ARMENIAN CONVENT—NEW PALACE, ETC.—CLERICAL SEMINARY—WALK ABOUT MOUNT ZION—CŒNACULUM—TOMB OF DAVID—CHRISTIAN CEMETERIES —ENGLISH BURIAL GROUND—VIEW FROM BROW OF ZION OVER TO THE TEMPLE—THE BRIDGE—WILLIAMS' PRETENDED CORRECTION, ETC.—THE JEWS IN JERUSALEM—THEIR QUARTER—CONDITION, ETC.—JEWISH DISPENSARY.

Formerly the traveller to Jerusalem had no choice but to put up at one of the convents, his servant providing his meals; or to take a lodging in some private house. At this period (1853) there are two inns, the "Mediterranean," and the "Maltese," where good rooms and fare are to be obtained, at an average charge of thirty-five to fifty piastres per day, according to rooms and table, including a supply of table-wine made in the neighbourhood; the best quality of which is really excellent. To insure comfort in a place like Jerusalem this charge cannot be considered exorbitant. Bottled ale and porter, with wines and spirits, may either be had at these houses as extras, or bought at the stores near the Jaffa Gate, and in Patriarch Street. These inns are often crowded in the winter and spring. Travellers desirous of greater privacy, or making a lengthened stay, may obtain decent lodgings without much difficulty,—certainly the most economical plan. Some persons still prefer to put up at the Casa Nuova, or new building erected at the Latin convent for the accommodation of all comers; where the rooms are said to be clean and comfortable. There is no fixed price; but an English traveller is expected to give a rather handsome compliment for the accommodation thus afforded. There he can either have his meals furnished by the convent cook, or prepared by his own servant; and most persons will with reason prefer the latter; and in this way the expense will be little less than living at one of the hotels. There are one or two persons acting as guides; but, like the monks, they are unintelligent retailers of the old traditions, of but little service; and a good map is of far greater use. In perambulating the city and environs, it is better for the traveller to be accompanied by his servant, both as a protection and to enable him to make any inquiries; and those who have arms will do well to carry them about in their suburban excursions, as the Arabs, if they see a stranger thus unprotected, are sometimes apt to be troublesome, though a trifling baksheesh is generally efficacious in disarming their opposition.

On passing through the deep archway of the Jaffa Gate and entering the city, we have, upon the left hand, an open space, irregularly terminated by buildings; and, on the right, the fosse and towers of "el Kalah," or, the Castle of David—the modern citadel. Before noticing this building at length, it should be pointed out, that at the angle of the above-mentioned open space, within the north-west angle of the city, are the ruins of an ancient building, called "Kasr Jalud," or Goliattiz Castle. Mr. Williams considers this as beyond doubt the tower mentioned in the history of the Crusaders' Siege, as that against which Tancred was encamped, and which was afterwards called by his

name; and he suggests, that it may have belonged to the third wall of Josephus.

It is on entering the city by this gate that one is chiefly struck with the progress of modern improvements. In fact this may be called figuratively no less than literally the "west-end" of the city. Several new shops greet the eye, in which may be found a great variety of European necessaries and comforts. A few new and, for Jerusalem, handsome buildings are erected, and the waste ruinous look of the place is giving way to something a little more modern and habitable. The two prominent objects that meet the eye are the ancient tower at the angle of the citadel, and the recently finished English church and consulate; nor would it be easy to point out two edifices more strikingly dissimilar in every respect. The stern massive masonry of the former, bearing evident marks of high antiquity, and encrusted with that mellow brown tint produced by time in this climate, forms a strong contrast with the light façade of English gothic, of white stone, as yet unstained, and glittering against the deep blue sky."

Between the citadel and the church is an open square, very badly paved, bordered with the new banking-house of M. Bergheim, a coffee-house and shops, and generally filled with groups of camels with their Arab conductors. Looking down upon this square is the house occupied by the Bishop, which, though internally comfortable, has nothing either palatial or ecclesiastical in its exterior to recommend it. The citadel, one of the most prominent buildings in the city, is of irregular form and of considerable extent, surrounded by a fosse, across which there is a bridge giving access through a gateway to the open square just mentioned. It is well-built and massive, occupying a bold position, looking down on the Valley of Hinnom. A few guns are mounted on its ramparts, and it affords a stronghold, sufficient at least to keep in check an irregular army unprovided with heavy artillery. Among its towers the most conspicuous is that already alluded to (and depicted in the view), distinguished from the others by the more ancient and massive character of its masonry. The stones of which it is composed, though on a smaller scale, have the same peculiarity as those in the Temple wall, and the inclosure of the mosque at Hebron, viz. the centre part is raised. Besides this characteristic of Jewish architecture, the lower part of the tower is solid; and these are circumstances which undoubtedly contribute to strengthen the conjecture of many archæologists who have written on the subject, that this is no other than the tower of Hippicus; one of the three noble bulwarks of the wall of Zion, which were left standing by Titus, as a shelter for the Roman camp, after the destruction of the rest of Jerusalem. But although we may safely assign a Jewish origin to this tower, yet that it was that of Hippicus is, after all, but a conjecture; and perhaps antiquarians have been a little too confident in assuming this point as one entirely settled, and making it the keystone, in fact, of the topography of the whole city.

The Anglican Cathedral Church, called Christ Church, owes its origin to the London Society for Promoting Christianity among the Jews. This institution was founded in 1809; but its first mission of inquiry to Palestine was not sent out till the year 1820. The Rev. Lewis Way visited the Holy Land with this object in 1823, and Dr. Dalton repaired to Jerusalem as Medical Missionary in 1824, but died in 1826. The Rev. J. Nicolayson arrived at the seat of his mission on the last day of December 1825, but two years afterwards was for a while compelled to return to England by political difficulties. During his absence the proposal for building a church at Jerusalem was just canvassed. But affairs of all kinds move slowly in the East, and it was not, therefore, till 1838 that the land was bought and some temporary buildings commenced. These had risen to the height of one story when Mr. Hillier arrived in Jerusalem as architect, but had scarcely begun operations, when he was cut off by an attack of fever. This fatality, with the breaking out of hostilities between the quadruple alliance and Mehemet Ali,

DIFFICULTIES OF THE FOUNDATION.

suspended for a while the progress of the work. This being terminated, Mr. J. W. Johns received the vacant appointment as architect, and arrived at Jerusalem in July 1841. Having completed his design, which was approved by the authorities, Mr. J. cleared away the old building, and began to lay the foundation of the church, with the intention, at first, of resting it upon a concrete foundation. "I was, however," he says, "soon convinced of the utter impossibility of *forming a foundation which could be depended upon of this material*, from the *honeycomb nature of the debris accumulated on the rock of this portion of Mount Zion*, from the numberless sieges and earthquakes Jerusalem has been subjected to, from the time when David wrested his stronghold from the Jebusites till the wars of Mehemet Ali, its late possessor. Such uncertainty of soil and rubbish existed, that you could not form any conjecture as to what the next blow of the pickaxe would alight upon. It was impossible to foresee whether it would be a portion of a *ruined chamber*, *loose rubbish*, some part of a *destroyed arch*, perhaps *in an inverted* position—a portion of a *broken floor*—or, as in some cases, a small portion of tolerably solid masonry, and if so this would probably rest upon *loose rubbish*. There was not, in fact, in any of the six large shafts sunk to the rock, *one foot of anything that could be depended on until we reached the maiden earth*, and this only remained undisturbed in two very small portions, where it formed only thin strata upon the rock—*all, all, is unsubstantial deposit of the razing siege or the destroying earthquake*. Finding such an unsolid substratum, I determined at once to proceed down to the rock, and thus obtain a foundation against which the rain might descend, and the storm beat without fear of its being moved. Accordingly, the shaft at the south-east angle was commenced and carried down to the solid rock, and on the 28th January, 1842, the first stone was laid by Bishop Alexander, on the rock of Mount Zion, at the depth of *thirty-five* feet from the surface. The other shafts were also sunk, the lowest point touched being no less than *thirty-nine feet* from the surface!

To lay the foundation proved to be the most laborious part of the business, the cubical contents of the whole amounting to 70,000 feet of masonry. When they were at length completed, on the 1st of November 1842, being All Saints Day, the first stone of the work above ground was laid by Mrs. Alexander. It continued to advance until the middle of January 1843, when, through the interference of the Turkish authorities, it was again brought to a stoppage. "The building had, up to this period, progressed upwards of five feet from the ground, and had attracted general attention, not so much from its ornamental appearance, as from the finish and exactness of the work, and the regularity of the bare mouldings. The natives seem to look upon exactness and neatness in building as things which cannot now be attained, and when they allude to the Saracenic and other buildings now existing in Jerusalem, they speak of them as works to be admired, but which they imagine modern art cannot accomplish."

In the course of his extensive excavations, Mr. Johns lighted upon an arched chamber, and what he believes to have been an aqueduct of very superior construction, of which a detailed account is given in "Walks about Jerusalem." By some this has been supposed to be a portion of a subterranean passage that is said to extend from the Temple to Mount Zion.

We may add to the constantly accumulating evidences of subterranean remains in the city, the following recently communicated by Dr. Barclay:—

"You remember," he writes, "Beit Renbina, an old ruined church a short distance north-east of the minaret in the Jewish quarter, and a few yards east of the Jewish bazaar. In digging foundations for a house between it and the street, the workmen came to quite a large gateway of massive stones (not Jewish in character), two indeed. One in a wall running nearly north and south. The other in a wall springing from it close by the gate, and running eastward—the former the larger. The *top of the arches* was only about eight or ten feet below the present surface of the earth."

Such were the difficulties encountered by Mr. Johns in laying a sure foundation for the English Church on Mount Zion—but he was not permitted to bring to a completion the work he had so successfully begun. This is a point too delicate to be entered into here, though we cannot hesitate to endorse the opinion of the Rev. Mr. Williams, that the architect was harshly treated—through what agency it is not our business to inquire. Another superintendent was appointed in his place, and the building apparently greatly altered from the original design as published in Mr. Johns's work, "The Anglican Cathedral Church of Saint James, Mount Zion." As there represented, the church was entirely detached; but at present the consulate is attached to it, giving to the whole rather the appearance of the moiety of a college, with its chapel or hall in the centre, and the other wing unfinished, than of a cathedral, or even of a parish church.

For this the architect is not to be blamed, as it seems since, in order to meet the requirements of Turkish law, it was necessary to erect a consulate, and consider the church as merely dependent upon it. Such were but so recently the degrading restrictions imposed by the Turks upon a power to which their establishment on the spot is owing, and which is now lavishing the national blood and treasure in endeavouring to prop up their imbecile and barbarian government. The operations of this Society, and the foundation of a church on Mount Zion paved the way to the establishment of an English Bishopric at Jerusalem. This is a measure of so peculiar and exceptional a character, and has been so often the subject of misunderstanding, that a brief explanation of its origin, derived from official sources, may not be undesirable. The proposal originated with the King of Prussia, and is contained in an instruction given to the

Chevalier Bunsen, his learned ambassador at the court of St. James.

This envoy was instructed to inquire, " In how far the English National Church, already in possession of a parsonage on the Mount Zion, and having commenced there the building of a church, would be inclined to accord to the Evangelical National Church of Prussia a sisterly position in the Holy Land." This proposal was warmly received by the Secretary for Foreign Affairs, as well as the Archbishop of Canterbury, and the Bishop of London, and the negotiation was speedily effected. It was stipulated that the English Bishop of Jerusalem was to be nominated alternately by the crowns of England and Prussia, the Archbishop having the absolute right of veto, with respect to those nominated by the Prussian crown. The jurisdiction of the Bishop was to extend over English clergy and congregations, and any who might join his church—in Palestine, Syria, Chaldea, Egypt, and Abyssinia. His chief missionary care was to be directed to the conversion of the Jews, to their protection, and to their useful employment. He was to establish and maintain as far as in him lies relations of Christian charity with other churches represented at Jerusalem, and in particular with the orthodox Greek Church; taking special care to convince them that the Church of England does not wish to disturb, or divide, or interfere with them; but that she is ready in the spirit of Christian love to render them such offices of friendship as they may be willing to receive. To this it is added, that German congregations are to be under the care of German clergymen ordained by the Bishop, and under his jurisdiction.

It is not to be supposed that an arrangement so peculiar and momentous as the preceding would pass without much hostile comment. An English Bishop half-appointed and chiefly paid by a German Lutheran monarch, sent out to preside over about half-a-dozen Englishmen in Jerusalem, and a few others scattered over a wide extent of territory—might well appear to the Orientals as being at least as much a political as a religious institution. And, notwithstanding the professions of the English primate to his dear brethren the Greeks and Latins—and, notwithstanding the zealous fraternization of his chaplain with the Oriental churches, and the candles which the latter is said to have carried in their services, these Oriental patriarchs could not but look with evil eye upon another prelate sent out to consolidate Protestantism, and obtain a share of that influence for which they were incessantly fighting. Many Protestants indeed conscientiously objected to intruding upon what appeared to be the diocese of another patriarch—though certainly without reason—as Jerusalem has been well called a free city for all religions; and Protestantism had as much right to take root there as any other form of Christianity.

The error, if any, was in making uncalled-for professions of amity with the Oriental churches, in not taking up from the first a totally independent position, and regarding the dissemination of the Scriptures, and any results that might follow, as being entirely in the power of the Bishop, whether it might trench or not upon the supposed prescriptive rights of the Eastern prelates, or have a tendency to call the attention of their flocks from the abuses and superstitions of their own creed to the genuine oracles of the Faith.

To provide an endowment for the bishopric, the King of Prussia undertook to make at once the munificent donation of 15,000*l.* towards that object, the annual interest of which, amounting to 600*l.*, is to be paid yearly in advance, till the capital sum, together with that which is to be raised by subscription, for the purpose of completing the Bishop's annual income of 1200*l.*, can be advantageously invested in land situate in Palestine.

In pursuance of this plan the Archbishop consecrated the Rev. Michael Solomon Alexander—himself a converted Jew—as first Bishop of the United Church of England and Ireland in Jerusalem. He was furnished with a Letter Commendatory from the primate to the right reverend our brothers in Christ, the prelates and bishops of the ancient and apostolic churches in Syria, and the countries adjacent, greeting in the Lord; and took out with him, as chaplain, the Rev. G. Williams, B. D., a fellow of King's College, Cambridge, who has since come forward so prominently as the champion of ecclesiastical tradition, against all who dare to impugn it.

Dr. Alexander was not privileged long to occupy the post to which he had been thus honourably inducted. He died in November 1845; when the Rev. S. Gobat, formerly missionary in Abyssinia, received the vacant appointment, and reached Jerusalem exactly a twelvemonth after the death of his respected predecessor. Such is a brief sketch of the origin and progress of the English Episcopate at Jerusalem.

On Sunday morning I repaired to the church on Mount Zion, before the commencement of service. This was the first time I had seen the interior, which, without any pretensions to architectural beauty or decorative elegance, is neat, plain, and sufficiently appropriate, presenting, in its chaste simplicity, a striking contrast to the tinsel splendour of the Greek church of the Holy Sepulchre. The congregation was far more numerous than I remembered it some years ago, shortly after the mission was founded; and the edifice, which is not large, was pretty respectably filled. Besides the families of the Bishop, the missionaries, and the consul, there were the female heads of the Jewish schools, with their young charge; numerous Jewish proselytes, and some miscellaneous hangers-on to the English interest in Jerusalem. The service was performed as in ordinary parish churches in England. There is a fine-toned organ, over which the consul's lady presided; and the musical part of the service was very admirably conducted.

On this Sunday a sermon was preached by Bishop Gobat, and on the next by a member of the Mission; the tone of whose discourse seemed, as I fancied, rather highflown and enthusiastic. From passages in both discourses, I was led to infer that expectations were entertained of some great change about to happen. Allusions, too, were made to much sickness and suffering among the missionary families. The Bishop himself had just lost one of his children, to whom the King of Prussia had stood godfather about a year before.

The Mission was at that moment labouring somewhat under discouragement. It was not long before that a sad rebuff was given to the clergyman above alluded to, who, in the exercise of a zeal, certainly more fervent than prudent, (and partly, as I was informed, at the invitation of certain Jewish proselytes,) had repaired to the Jewish quarter, to preach the Gospel in the open street—a proceeding, I understood, rather permitted than suggested by the Bishop. Supported by some of his friends, he had scarcely begun his address, when certain of the Rabbis, infuriated at this open inroad upon their flock, instigated their followers to drive him from the spot with a storm of stones and dead cats; and at the solicitation of a Turkish official, who was afraid that a riot would be the consequence, he was obliged to retire with his party. However disgraceful this violence, it was surely not a little imprudent thus to arouse the fanaticism of the Jews, and throw fresh fuel on the flame of religious discord, of which Jerusalem appears ever to have been the chosen seat,—compromising the national dignity, and affording amusement to the hostile Greeks and Latins.

Nor less to be regretted is the injudicious zeal of others, who, in their haste to "give a lift to the Mission," have been led to receive proselytes whose character has reflected upon it nothing but disgrace. It must not be supposed that this reproach is intended to apply to the Mission in general, who are sincerely desirous of receiving none but genuine converts, and such whose behaviour testifies to the sincerity of their conviction; though, of course, it is impossible to read the heart of every proselyte, or, even if his conversion is perhaps sincere, to answer for the consistency of his conduct.

The following details, from official sources, may not be uninteresting in addition:—

The church contains sittings for about 200 persons. The late Miss Cook contributed £4,600 to the building; besides which, that lady gave £8,500, as a perpetual endowment. The Rev. J. Nicolayson, who had previously laboured many years as a missionary in Jerusalem, holds the appointment of minister.

The church is now used as a cathedral church of the Anglican bishopric of Syria, Chaldea, Egypt, and Abyssinia.

The Anglican services are as follow: at 10 A.M. every Sunday morning, and on the principal festivals. The same in the German language every second Sunday, at 3 P.M.; and the same in Hebrew, every morning at 6 in summer and 7 in winter; besides the Communion Service in Arabic, every Sacrament Sunday early.

The London Society has permitted evangelical congregations of foreign communities to worship in its church, under certain regulations agreed upon between the Trustees and the Bishop; accordingly the Prussian congregation, under the Rev. F. Valentiner, at present avail themselves of this permission in the afternoon of every second Sunday.

The sacramental vessels, with Hebrew inscriptions, had been already in use in Jerusalem, the produce of a subscription from the ladies of Reading; an additional paten was added by W. Stephen, Esq., of Reading, in 1845. A carpet for the chancel was a present from some English ladies, of their own handiwork. The church books were purchased by a subscription from the Sunday schools of Bristol. The organ was a donation recently made by the widow of the Rev. W. M. Barnes, M.A.; and a beautifully carved alms-basin was presented by W. G.

Rogers, Esq., of London, the celebrated artist in wood, in 1851.

The census of the congregation, taken in Sept. 1853, was as follows:—

	Adults.	Children.
Anglicans	34	18
Jewish proselytes	32	27
Jewish catechumens	19	7
Arab communicants	20	22
Prussian congregation	21	2
Total	126	76

besides some children in the Diocesan schools not belonging to parents of the above classes.

In a small range of buildings near the church are the offices of the English consulate, and the library belonging to the Literary Society of Jerusalem, an institution at present in its infancy, but which is probably destined to render no small aid to the cause of scientific inquiry in Palestine, besides tending to diffuse among the society of the city a taste for intellectual enjoyments, and topics for social converse, and furnishing the traveller with the welcome resource of a library of reference and amusement. The institution was founded on Nov. 20, 1849, under the following distinguished auspices:—

> *Patrons.*—His Grace the Archbishop of Canterbury.
> Right Honourable Earl of Aberdeen, K.T., F.R.S.
> *Vice-Patron.*—Right Rev. Lord Anglican Bishop of Jerusalem.
> *Presidents.*—J. Finn, Esq., M.R.A.S., H. B. M. Consul.

This association has (besides the local members) corresponding members throughout the country, and foreign corresponding members, of literary eminence, in Britain, Germany, United States, India, and Central Asia.

A library of nearly a thousand volumes has been collected, chiefly from English contributors, with a small museum, which contains some interesting objects of antiquity and natural history;

and a handsome sun-dial has been erected by the Society, adjoining the church.

Literary meetings for reading of papers are held, for several months in the year, on Friday evenings, at the Consulate-house. The Society, it is understood, is anxious to form a collection of scientific instruments, for the use of persons intending to prosecute researches.

The territorial limits to which this Society confines its investigations, are those of the Mediterranean to the Euphrates, and the mouths of the Nile to the Orontes.

A peculiarity of its constitution is, that the writing members by whom opinions are expressed must be Protestants and Christians residing in the Holy Land, although the use of the library and museum is open to all persons of whatever nation or religion. This restriction is considered expedient only inasmuch as the place is Jerusalem, where it is impossible to touch upon antiquities or history without at the same time awakening the consideration of theological doctrines, concentrated as these are in that country upon peculiar localities, and, alas! environed by polemical controversy! The founders judged that upon no other principle could a literary society *in Jerusalem* ensure freedom of opinion, while they allow access of all to their repositories of means for acquiring knowledge.

The register of members contains names from a great diversity of nations over the world.

A plot of ground has been set apart, at a short distance from the city, for botanical purposes, attached to the Society, but for want of funds this has turned to small account as yet.

His Majesty the King of Prussia has bestowed upon the association the unconditional use of the library to be established in the Evangelical Hospice.

The establishment of such an institution as this in the city where Christianity originated, and which has so long been sunk in ignorance and barbarism, is among the most interesting signs of the times. Besides the number of accomplished men in Jerusalem who form the centre of the Society, there are few travellers who do not revert with interest to their sojourn in the Holy Land, and when returned to the more engrossing pursuits of home, desire to keep up a connexion with the East. In such a Society those blessed with the possession of wealth or intellectual superiority find a ready medium of communication with Jerusalem friends, and maintain a fellowship of art and science which would languish if confined to mere private communications, instead of diffusing increasing light and intelligence among the Orientals.

The objects and prospects of the Society are best expressed by a short extract from an address of the learned president:—

"But the very existence of such an association would be regarded as an impossibility by those who only knew Jerusalem as it was a few years ago. How very short a period has elapsed since this city, with its holy and spirit-stirring history, and its wondrous prospects in prophecy, presented but the anomalous appearance of an Arab village, enclosed indeed with crenelled walls, like those of fortresses in the middle ages of Europe, but governed by an Arab peasant, Shaikh, or a Bash Bezuk Aza. That period has gone and never can return. The political diplomacy of European nations now brought to bear upon Jerusalem, the resident Patriarchates, and the religious missions of various kinds centred here, all forbid the recurrence of such humiliation. May I not also add in the presence of this large assembly, convoked in the name of literature, history, and science, having our outposts of eminent men in sundry parts of the globe, who are gratified at being incorporated with us, that we too have a part in upholding Jerusalem from a relapse into the condition which we just described in the pages of Chateaubriand and Lamartine.

"Still there are those in Europe who cannot bring themselves to believe that this country is as yet sufficiently settled or civilized to warrant the undertaking of our object; but they forget that the order and improvement of a people are the effects of institutions found among them. It is because there are patriarchates, bishoprics, consulates, hospitals, printing presses, and libraries, that the city and country acquire the character which such establishments confer. These, becoming grounded into the very framework of social existence, here not only have their several independent modes of action, but reflect influence upon each other, and upon the prior and local institutions. From the whole of these brought together there is undoubtedly a real civilization in progress amongst us in names and opinions.

"It is not without some effect that the city is seldom or never without the presence of some well-informed travellers remaining for a shorter or longer period; and still more, that the clerical seminary of the Greek community is raising up a generation of youths versed in the highest range of the classic poets, philosophers, and historians, both Greek and Latin, as well as in modern languages. The effect of this cannot fail to be perceived in a very few years.

"The Latin Patriarchate is supplied with men of erudition and talent.

"It will be observed, however, that the improvement in Jerusalem is all on the side of Europeanism, for Arabic and Hebrew studies pursue their mere monotonous circuit.

"Enough has been said to show that this is no longer the barbarous place it has been; and that with such topics and materials as Palestine affords from itself, our undertaking was not premature in its commencement.

"But there are friends to our cause in Europe who rejoice in the enterprise, and have assisted the formation of our library and museum, under the conviction that this city (irrespective of its transcendent religious importance) is suited to become the centre of civilization to Asia, and who can participate in the bold belief, that even the establishment here of a universal library in combination with a series of kindred institutions, would be an object worthy the attention of the most eminent scholars, and need not be undeserving the patronage of crowned monarchs.

"Time, however, will ripen into their appropriate fruits those gems which have already tinged with hopeful green the aspect of this Oriental wilderness. The generation after us will see greater changes in the general and particular circumstances in Palestine than we have witnessed since the days of our immediate fathers. We now watch the sprouting up as it were of some new germinations from a soil long regarded as exhausted and abandoned by God and man; but our successors will enjoy the shade of spreading trees, for which we have planted the acorns. It is this consideration alone which imparts a serious importance to our work, and renders the association suited to engage the endeavours of rational man."

Whatever may be thought of the principle, in a religious point of view, of this Mission, one thing is certain, it has undeniably promoted the cause of European civilization in Jerusalem. Wherever the English establish themselves, they never fail to introduce a higher standard of comfort, improved sanitary regulations, to give a stimulus to industry and agriculture. The neighbouring peasantry find their account in this new state of things, and are increasingly sensible that their interests are interwoven with those of the Franks. They get not only a better market, but better prices also. But this increase of animal comforts is the lowest result that has followed the settlement of the English. A feeling of rivalry on the part of other sects has led them to emulate the educational measures of the Mission, and a general activity has succeeded to the stagnant torpor of ignorance and sloth, that has so long settled over the Eastern churches. The society of the place has been enlarged and improved. The consulates of the principal foreign powers are no longer filled up by Syrians, but by educated and often distinguished natives of the different countries represented, who form an intellectual and refined circle; so that in winter, when the city is visited by numerous travellers, as many as fifty or sixty invitations have been issued for an evening party at the consulate. The Franks in the city are now every way in the ascendant; their numbers and influence are continually on the increase, while in both respects the Turks are as steadily losing ground. It should be mentioned, in connexion with the increasing influence of the Christians, that the government of Jerusalem has been changed from that of a simple Arab Mutsellim to a Turkish Pashalic, expressly to protect more efficaciously the various Christian interests of Turkish subjects. The first Turkish Pasha arrived from Constantinople Dec. 1, 1840, with the rank of Ferik,—since which the Pashalic has been raised in rank twice.

Such are a few of the indirect results springing from the establishment of the Mission at Jerusalem. But these results are so clearly traced in a communication kindly forwarded by the accomplished lady of the British Consul, that I cannot do better than lay it in full before the reader.

JERUSALEM IN ITS MODERN ASPECT, BY A SEVEN YEARS' RESIDENT.

THE various descriptions given of life and manners in the Holy City during the last few years are scarcely less opposed to each other than are those handed down to us by the Sacred Historians, Josephus, Crusading chroniclers, monkish recluses, and pilgrims. While some have been heard to exclaim that over the gates should be inscribed, 'Lasciate ogni speranza voi ch' entrate!' others gratefully sing, "Jerusalem, my happy home." Every prospect is more or less tinged by the mind of the observer, and every object takes its proportions according to the point of view whence it is regarded. But with Jerusalem this has been and is preeminently the case.

The aged Hebrew pilgrim, arriving weary and destitute at the goal of his earthly wanderings, distinguishes not between the domes of the Holy Sepulchre and those of the Mohammedan mosques. To him the Gothic architecture of the English church and the glistening front of the Armenian patriarchate are alike strongholds of the Goyim (Gentiles); and whether Christian bells waft their magician sounds[1] over the crowded dwellings of Zion, or the Muezzins " cry aloud" from the minaret, as did the prophets of Baal in olden time, his hope deferred, he exclaims, " Lord, how long ?"

The fashionable traveller, on the other hand, satiate with the charms of Italy, weary of the Alps and the Black Forest, seeks Oriental excitement and western civilization on the banks of the Nile, or the desolate hills of Judea, and lisps out his disappointment that there are no trees or water in Jerusalem, while the hotels are *very* inferior. He rails at the fanaticism which excludes him from the only pretty spot (the Mosque enclosure), and boasts, that two days " have done the Mount of Olives, the Wailing Place, Bethlehem, the Greek Fire, and all that." Such persons leave the Holy City without a suspicion of the earnest men and women who have here found a home and heart-stirring employment, where vacancy and ennui enter not.

But there are those, and they may be numbered by thousands, who reverently approach the sacred wall of Jerusalem in order to worship at the Holy Tomb—whose stedfast gaze is fixed upon the cupolas of the Church of the Resurrection, within whose precincts they intend to pass most of the time allotted for their sojourn in Jerusalem. Of the city they know nothing, and learn nothing but what may be seen in the convent where they sleep at night, and in the streets through which they must daily pass to and from the church. Even the more intelligent of the European travellers who visit Jerusalem at the season of Easter, are so occupied with the ceremonies to be seen or joined in, and the hurried visits to Bethlehem, Jordan, &c., that they must leave

[1] The Jews believe there is power of enchantment in Christian bells and church organs.

Palestine utterly ignorant of the present state of society, manners, and feelings in the Holy City. Some who attend the services in Christ Church on Mount Zion are surprised to find a numerous congregation, with their bishop, priests, and deacons, offering the well-known prayers and praises of the Church of England Liturgy, in the English language, and with the propriety and order so dearly prized at home. But what this congregation is, and why here assembled, few appear to know. Should the traveller be furnished with introductions to the English bishop, the minister, the consul, the physician, or others, he will probably find himself some evening in either of their houses, amid a numerous assemblage, perhaps some forty or fifty, whom he will be told are residents in Jerusalem. Interesting conversation, carried on in French, German, Italian, English, &c., and perhaps a little music, with every appearance of European comfort, may prompt the question, " Is this really Jerusalem; where everything has been described as so barbarous? What has brought all these people here? and what are they doing?"

Directly or indirectly, *Religious interest in the Holy City* has been the motive which has collected together so large a number of intelligent Europeans. The various gentlemen of the assemblage are either attached to the English Episcopate, or to the Prussian Mission, or agents of Missionary Societies, or officers of the various Consulates. These, with their ladies, form a large circle, besides other persons of independent fortune who have chosen the Holy City as their home; and it sometimes happens that travellers prolong their visits for several months. Thus a numerous and superior society may at all times be found in Jerusalem.

But how has *Religious interest* brought all these people thither?

Let us go back a very few years, and we shall find the only European resident in the Holy City was the Rev. John Nicolayson, stationed there by an apparently insignificant religious Society "for Promoting Christianity among the Jews." An American Mission to the Gentiles was also attempted, but its success did not encourage the continuance of this effort in Jerusalem.

Two or three families of Jewish converts had scarcely gathered round Mr. Nicolayson before the Society in England made preparations for building a church, and establishing an hospital, in order to exhibit Christianity fully to the eyes of the Jewish population. Other plans for schools, colleges, houses of industry, &c., were announced. The Egyptian government was not unfavourable to European movement, and permitted the *actual* purchase of land on Mount Zion; but even with this advantage, the schemes thus coolly planned for a fanatic and totally barbarous city and country seem sufficiently bold, and they appear to have attracted the attention of the government at home, if we may judge by the appointment of an English vice-consul to protect British interest. The native authorities were puzzled at the appearance among them of an officer whose duties and position they could scarcely understand; but whose immediate care was the protection of British property, and of such travellers as might visit Jerusalem.

A physician (in 1838), and soon afterwards an architect, commenced their labours; the former among the starving and dying Jewish population, and the latter in planning and commencing a handsome gothic building on the summit of Mount Zion. At the restoration of Palestine to Turkish government in 1840, the attention of Europe was turned towards that country, and in 1841 what appeared a most extraordinary appointment was made by Prussia and England. A Jerusalem bishopric was founded, and the Bishop consecrated at Lambeth, Nov. 1841. To send a Bishop where there was no congregation, appeared to many a piece of folly second only to the presumption of intruding upon the ecclesiastical rights already existing in the Holy City. Precedents, however, for securing to each community its ecclesiastical head, were not wanting in the Armenian, Syrian, Coptic, and Latin communities, and the right to appoint over their respective congregations superiors of the highest rank has since been claimed and exercised by the Latins, and Greek Catholics, in the sending to Jerusalem their patriarchs, and by the Russians for their Archimandrate.

But a reference to the documents put forth at the time by those immediately concerned, will show that his majesty the King of Prussia, who originated the idea, was anxious to benefit a numerous class; certainly not under the immediate jurisdiction of either Greek, Latin, or Armenian convents. He has for years regarded the Jewish people with deep interest, and was desirous of consolidating the Mission to them already begun. His majesty further desired to set before the ancient Oriental churches the example of a completely constituted Protestant Church, and to provide in an effectual manner for the spiritual wants of his own subjects in the East. The following extracts give an interesting view of the king's intentions:—" At the present moment, more especially, may we not presume it to be an object dear to the Great Head of the Church himself, that the Land of Promise, and the scene of his earthly pilgrimage, should behold Israel brought to know his great salvation? Neither this alone, but that the several churches of Protestantism, whose foundations are laid in the everlasting Gospel, and upon the rock of that faith which confesses the Son of the living God, should, forgetting their divisions, call their oneness to remembrance, and standing over the sepulchre of the Redeemer, hold out to each other the right hand of peace and unity. . . . .

" But, above all things, his majesty is determined to make every effort in the Holy Land, which can on Christian principles be required of him towards promoting in common concert the interests of the Gospel. The Church of England is in possession of an ecclesiastical foundation on Mount Zion, and his majesty deems it, therefore, the duty of every Protestant prince and community to attach themselves to this foundation, as the starting and central point of combined efforts. . . . . . His majesty esteems it to be the first condition and step towards such an unity of action, that *the Church of England should institute a Bishopric at Jerusalem*. The foundation for it is, as if by a special act of Providence, already laid. . . . . The episcopate to be instituted at Jerusalem would associate itself with the institutions and erections on Mount Zion, and include all Protestant Christians in the Holy Land within its pale, so far as they should be disposed to take part in it."[1] . . . .

The Bishop was, therefore, commended to the Oriental Christians, with directions to show them all friendliness, and to avoid encroaching upon their rights, while he was yet free to accept under his jurisdiction all those who should "join his church, and place themselves under his episcopal authority in Palestine."[2]

The Right Rev. M. S. Alexander, a Hebrew Christian, left England in Dec. 1841, accompanied by his numerous family, his chaplains, the recently appointed physician, &c. &c., and entered Jerusalem January 20, 1842.

At this period Jerusalem was destitute of every European comfort, and a very inferior Oriental city. The markets were ill-supplied with meat; there was no milk, but few vegetables, and none but Arab bread; not a common plate or cup, or chair or table to be got; no carpenter, no butcher, no baker, no washerwoman, and, worst of all, no servants—no glass in the windows to keep out the winter rain or snow and piercing winds. The influx of so large a number of Europeans, however, soon wrought great changes in these respects; and it was not long before all the necessaries of life and many foreign luxuries were procurable.

---

[1] Instructions of the King of Prussia to his ambassador, M. Bunsen, Sans Souci, 2 June, 1841, as given in "The Protestant Bishopric in Jerusalem," London: Wertheim, pp. 46, 49—51.

[2] See Statement of Proceedings relating to the establishment of a Bishopric of the United Church of England and Ireland at Jerusalem.

Shortly after the arrival of the Bishop, the former British vice-consul returned with the rank of consul. Not long before had been appointed the first Turkish Pasha, to protect the (native) Christian interests at Jerusalem. The only ecclesiastical dignitaries of high rank in the Holy City at this time were the Syrian bishop, the Armenian patriarch, and the Greek metropolitan bishop. The Greek patriarch of Jerusalem always resided in Constantinople. The rising importance of the Holy City was marked by the establishment, in 1843, of Prussian, Sardinian and French consulates, held by natives of the respective countries, men of talent and influence. The Greek patriarch arrived in 1846, and took up his residence in Jerusalem. Then followed the Greek Catholic patriarch, and the Latin patriarch. Churches were repaired or rebuilt, and houses erected for the accommodation of these personages. About this time also the Russian Archimandrate had taken up his residence as chief of the Russian Church in Jerusalem.

An Austrian consulate was founded in 1849, to which Count Pizzamano, a military man of rank and talent, was appointed.

The first Anglican Bishop died in 1845, on his way to England; and his successor, the Right Rev. Samuel Gobat, (late principal of the Protestant college at Malta, and formerly missionary in Abyssinia,) was appointed by the King of Prussia. The appointment is exercised alternately by England and Prussia.

The establishment by this prelate of a Diocesan school, in which were taught boys and girls of all creeds and nations, Jews, Moslems, Christians—Copts, Greeks, and Latins—children of Hebrew converts to Christianity, and of German and English parents—the establishment of this school speedily gave an impulse to education, and schools for girls, under the supervision of Sisters of Charity, and for boys, were opened by the Latin patriarch, and have been very well attended. The Greeks also could no longer resist the progress of events, and opened their schools. Both of these communities have now (1853) upper schools, or seminaries, in which young men receive classic and general education under European masters. The Greek upper school contains fifty scholars, and the day school numbers ninety, with four masters in the latter. Even the Armenians, an exclusive and thoroughly Oriental community, have added to their enormous convent a fine building with separate apartments, for the accommodation of twenty young men, who are here to receive a seven years' training. It is to be hoped that the effort which is now being made to reestablish the English college will be supported. Having formerly set the example to others, the English have at this moment no college in Jerusalem, but it cannot be supposed that this state of things is to continue.

The Medical Mission of the above-named Jews' Society has been perhaps one of the most beneficial efforts made for the good of Jerusalem. The hospital, where several hundred in-door and several thousand out-door cases are annually relieved, has been a direct benefit to the poor Jews; and was for several years the only source of medical aid for the whole city. This is, however, no longer the case. The medical provision made for the Jews by Sir Moses Montefiore, the hospital of the Latin patriarchate, the dispensaries of the Latin and Greek convents (the latter admirably furnished), the hospital and dispensary of the Prussian deaconesses, the semi-medical mission of Dr. Barclay, an American, and the number of private practitioners, prevent the possibility of such a sad scene as Mr. Nicolayson's house presented in 1834, when his family and the American missionaries were all ill of fever, and unable to aid each other. Providentially the officers and surgeon of an English ship at Jaffa came up to visit Jerusalem, and assisted the sufferers. There were recently no fewer than eight Frank M.D.'s residing in Jerusalem.

Several printing-presses are in active operation in the Holy City; but, strange to say, the very superior press and types belonging to the English Mission have never yet been used. Meanwhile thousands of volumes are annually printed, bound and circulated by the Armenians in their own language; by the Latins, in Arabic and Italian. The Greek convent has also a fine press at work. The Jewish press is not at present in use, but has been the means of multiplying copies of Hebrew controversial works against Christianity. The American Protestant mission at Beyroot has a very large and effective printing establishment, whence useful and popular books in Arabic are sent forth, and gladly read by the native Syrians. Some of these find their way to Jerusalem.

The various older communities live quite independently of, and have but little intercourse with, each other. First, in antiquity if not in interest, stands the remnant of Israel, which still clings with tenacious faith to the covenant made with Abraham nearly 4,000 years ago. The Jews are also the most numerous body in Jerusalem, and there is good reason to believe that their total number is about 11,000; divisible into Sephardim and Ashkenazim. The latter, or German and Polish Jews, are about 4,000. Their numbers are augmented by constant arrivals from Europe. Their principal support is derived from the money collected in the European synagogues, and which is sufficient for an allowance of about 1*l*. 10*s*. per annum for each person. Most of those who yearly arrive have spent their little savings on the journey, and trust to this fund and to any trade they may know for a livelihood. But these hopes are cruelly disappointed; 1*l*. 10*s*. per annum is a pitiful income in a place where water costs from threepence to fivepence per donkey load of four gallons, and the majority of this people are compelled to buy water during a great part of the year. A trade is useless where there is no employment. The Jews are too poor to employ each other. Moslems are willing to take their goods at a price fixed by themselves, or for no price at all. Native Christians avoid Jews as they would the plague, though of late a very few are beginning to regard them as in some sense their fellow-creatures; still it is most common to hear the apology,

"Bá'eed ának" (be it far from you), after the mention of a Jew, as well as after the mention of shoes or other things, whose very name is avoided. The English and other Europeans are indebted to Jewish artisans for the supply of almost all their wants, yet so small a community cannot give employment to several thousand people. An effort has been made to offer agricultural employment to the industrious and yet starving population. It is desired that some would find employment at Meshullam's farm at Urtass near Bethlehem, and others at the Industrial Plantation for Jews near Jerusalem. The latter of these institutions is yet in its infancy, and the proprietor of the former can scarcely do more than attend to the wants of his numerous family, although with wise fellow-workers much might be done.

The Sephardi, or Spanish community, numbers six to seven thousand, and includes first the descendants of those Jews expelled from Spain by Ferdinand and Isabella in the fifteenth century, many of whom found a refuge in Jerusalem among the Moslems. The Morocco and other Oriental Jews also belong to this division. Not only have the majority of these Jews no trades, but they have no allowance from the fund of the community, which is burthened with an increasing debt of two million piastres, about 20,000*l*. The money collected abroad is not enough to pay the interest upon this debt, which is about 15*l*. per day. Every Friday the synagogue servants go to the houses of those few who are a little better off, and beg loaves of bread, which they then distribute among the most needy. The disease and suffering occasioned by bad food, close crowded dwellings, and scarcity of water, are beyond description, and would surely, if known, awaken the compassion and active benevolence of happy England. Any one of the medical residents could testify that death from starvation is not uncommon. A well-directed system of employment is what would more than anything raise the poor Israelites of Zion from their mental and bodily degradation. The chief rabbi and head of both divisions must be a Sephardi; and the Spanish Jews generally despise and dislike the Ashkenazim. Each class has its own synagogues, rabbis, and councils, and all are tyrannised over and kept in bondage by those rabbis who hesitate at no means of keeping up their authority. The system which places the common fund at the sole disposal of the rabbis, together with the dread that the people entertain of the spiritual power (and especially of the excommunications) of these self-constituted rulers, gives them immense strength. Though, therefore, the Jews are beginning to look upon the English mission more favourably than formerly,—though they are in some cases beginning to understand that the worship of the Cross (the very form of idolatry for which they suppose the Canaanites to have been expelled) is not practised by Protestant Christians,—though moreover rabbinic excommunications can no longer deter Israelites from seeking medical relief at the hospital, or employment from those who will bestow it,—yet no sooner is a Jew suspected of a leaning towards Christianity, than he is exposed to severe persecution; his allowances are withdrawn, his wife persuaded to demand a divorce, his children stolen away from him, and himself exposed to personal violence in many cases. The Jews speak Hebrew among themselves, and the Ashkenazim have a dialect of German, and the Sephardim a dialect of Spanish in common use. The Oriental Jews also speak Arabic and several other languages.

The Christians, *i. e.* Latins, Greeks, Armenians, Copts, and Abyssinians, cluster round their respective convents. The Armenians are, perhaps, the most wealthy and contented. Evidently foreigners speaking their own language, but also well acquainted with Turkish, if not Arabic, they are a thriving and shrewd people,—keen in the acquisition of money, and intent on preserving their gains. Their convent on Mount Zion has been enlarged, and is now capable of accommodating 8,000 pilgrims. It is like a little fortified town; and the patriarchal palace, added to the other buildings, is one of the most commanding objects in the view of Jerusalem. The number of resident Armenians is small, though the number of pilgrims amounts to several thousands annually. The Copts are a very small body, residing in the convent which they possess attached to the Holy Sepulchre church. So also the Abyssinians, who regard Bishop Gobat as their friend and counsellor as well as ecclesiastical chief, and who remember with affection his former missionary efforts in Abyssinia. The Syrian or Jacobite bishop has a still smaller flock, consisting of about ten individuals. The Greek Catholics are not numerous, but their new church and Patriarchal residences are among the best modern buildings in Jerusalem, and justify the reputation for successful industry which the members of this body possess throughout Syria. The patriarch has been absent many months, his seat being at Damascus.

By far the largest native community is that of the orthodox Greeks, under the care of their patriarch, metropolitan, and other bishops. During the agitation at Constantinople respecting the Sacred Places, the patriarch has been at the capital, and his duties in the Holy City have devolved upon the metropolitan bishop—no unimportant charge, whether we regard the superintendence of the various convents, and of the subordinate clergy, the care of their congregations, including aid and advice in almost all their temporal concerns—or the oversight of the college schools, the providing both spiritually and temporally for the wants of four or five thousand pilgrims, many of whom spend four, five, or six months in Jerusalem; and also the oversight of the neighbouring establishments at the convent of the Cross, St. Saba, Bethlehem, &c. &c.

The Russian community under the Archimandrite Porphyrius, has gradually formed itself into a distinct though not entirely separate body. Its numbers are small but increasing. The hereditary rivals of the Greeks in Jerusalem and the adjacent sanctuaries, present no mean front in the Holy City. The Latin patriarch appears as the spiritual head of an active and intelligent class of Arab Christians, who have had hitherto much more idea of European civilization than their Greek and Armenian countrymen. Until 1848 the Franciscan and Carmelite monks were the only representatives in Palestine of the Latin church, and these were in general an ignorant and rude body of men, who were mostly sent to Palestine as a species of political banishment from Italy and Spain. Now, however, the monks are a superior class, and they are no longer looked upon as the representatives of the Latin church. The Italian and French secular clergy attendant on the patriarch, and the Sisters of Charity, have taken the lead; and the hospital, college, and schools under their care have added much to the weight of Romish influence. In the Roman Catholic circle of Jerusalem must be included the officers of the French consulate, under M. Botta, whose Nineveh discoveries have made for him a European reputation; also the officers of the Austrian consulate under Count Pizzamano. It is reported in the newspapers, that a Spanish consul is about to be sent to the Holy City. This is not improbable, as most of the monks and some laymen are Spaniards by birth, and large money contributions are annually sent from Spain.

The Protestant community, under the care of the Anglican Bishop, may be described under two heads: the Prussian and the English, each having its minister and distinct congregation. The Rev. J. Valentiner, who with his family arrived in Jerusalem in 1852, was sent thither by his Majesty the King of Prussia, as pastor to the congregation, numbering, in 1853, twenty-three persons, already formed in the Holy City, by the settlement of several German families, and the establishment of (under four deaconesses) their hospice, hospital and school. This respectable and thriving portion of his majesty's subjects are protected by their consul, Dr. G. Rosen, recently of the embassy at Constantinople, a worthy successor of the lamented Schultz, whose work on Jerusalem has proved so valuable an acquisition to the student of its antiquities. Christ Church is lent for the use of the Prussian congregation on the afternoon of every second Sunday. The English community formed, as we have seen, by the settlement of a solitary missionary nearly thirty years ago, has expanded and strengthened; and her British Majesty's consulate has now to protect several native English families with children of all ages, and single persons. Those of the congregation actually born in England, are twenty-six, with nine children. The Anglican Bishop is at the head of the Church Missionary establishment (whose centre of action for the Levant was transferred to Jerusalem in 1850). This mission is principally directed to the instruction and care of those Oriental Christians who have been expelled from the Greek and Latin churches, or who have voluntarily left them, because they exercised liberty to study the Scriptures in their own tongue, and desired teaching in conformity with what they thus learned. The number of native Protestants in Jerusalem is forty-two—twenty adults and twenty-two children—and they have congregations in Bethlehem, Jaffa, Nablous, Nazareth, &c. Arab Scripture-readers and schoolmasters are employed in the absence of English clergy, to devote themselves to their instruction. The Rev. F. Kléim is stationed at Nazareth, and the Rev. F. Kruse at Nablous. An Arabic service is held in Christ Church on every sacrament Sunday, by the Rev. J. Nicholayson, who is also head of the establishment of the London Society for Promoting Christianity amongst the Jews. This consists of a missionary staff under the Rev. J. Nicholayson, a House of Industry, for the employment of Hebrew converts, and a medical staff under E. Macgowan, Esq. M.D. who, together with a surgeon, apothecary, steward, &c., work the noble hospital for the relief of poor Jews. The Rev. H. Crawford is clerical missionary. Many of the Hebrew converts have settled in other countries, some as clergymen, schoolmasters, and artisans, and others live in Jerusalem, and form the Hebrew congregation. For these there are daily morning prayers of the Anglican liturgy in Hebrew, and on every second Sunday afternoon Anglican prayers and sermon in the German language; besides a service in Spanish on Sunday at the house of the Rev. H. Crawford. The English congregation, including the Hebrew converts, (sixty-six adults, forty-five children,) and the native English, assemble in Christ Church at ten o'clock every Sunday morning—when full service is held in English, with those hymns and chants that every child in England knows so well. The communicants are generally about fifty. Besides these services, there is a monthly missionary meeting in the school-room, and a Bible meeting in the Bishop's house. The diocesan schools for girls and boys are under the immediate control of the Bishop; the former numbers twenty-four, the latter between forty and fifty.

Among the independent institutions are the Schools of Industry, where fifty Jewesses are taught sewing by Miss Cooper and her assistant; and the Literary Society, with museum and library, President, H. B. M.'s Consul, in whose house weekly meetings are held during the winter season. Distinct from the above Protestant community is the Mission of the American Baptist sect, "The Disciples of Christ," who have stationed in Jerusalem the Rev. J. Barclay, M. D. with his family. He has made some converts, and holds services in his own house on Sundays, but the congregation is not large.

The various communities are rendered more compact by a circumstance which is, however, a serious disadvantage, and which time and the progress of events cannot fail to affect. The dependence of the poorer members of each is notorious, and this dependence often amounts to pauperism; and where it does not, still the servile bondage is most injurious, in which are held Greek, Latin, and Armenian Christians by their various convents, and the Jews by the Rabbis. The convents are proprietors generally of all the houses belonging to their people; they can therefore in a moment eject any person who becomes obnoxious to their displeasure, besides cutting off the allowances of clothing, food, medicine, &c. We have seen that the Jews can do even more. Though amongst the English missions every encouragement is given to independent industry, yet it often happens that the converts have no trade, and must be supported until they can learn one; or that they are old and helpless, cast out of house and home, and have just claims upon the temporal as well as spiritual charities of the missionaries.

The increasing number, however, of European residents adds to the probability that many, if not all, may eventually find useful employment, and be no longer either burdensome to or dependent upon others.

The foregoing facts will serve to show, that while other cities in the Turkish empire are falling to ruin and decay, being depopulated and barbarized, Jerusalem is rapidly springing up into new life. European manners and European wants are bringing in civilization and enterprising industry. Good hotels are found to accommodate most travellers better than the Casa Nuova, so long the only shelter for the Frank pilgrim of whatever nation or religion. There are shops, where all kinds of European goods find a ready sale for their commodities; carpenters, watchmakers, blacksmiths, glaziers, tinmen, dyers, laundresses, shoemakers, &c. exercise their various callings. There are three flourishing European tailors. The daily markets are supplied abundantly with good mutton; and poultry and eggs are cheap. Many hundred goats are kept for the sole purpose of supplying the city with milk; and of late, cow's milk is to be had. Fruit and vegetables are abundant; and good bread is made by several bakers.

New houses spring up on every side. By new houses[1] are

---

[1] Among these new houses may be reckoned the Mediterranean Hotel, in Christian-street; Antonio's Hotel; Messrs. Bergheim and Co.'s Bank, in Castle-square; the various extensive patriarchal residences; the house of the Russian archimandrite; the Austrian consulate, and many private houses.

The

meant new fabrics upon old foundations; for as yet the waste places are not reclaimed, and one-half the ancient city is a desolation, while other parts are over-crowded. The Frank quarter is chiefly from Mount Zion and the Jaffa Gate to the Damascus Gate; but, of late years, a good many houses have been taken in the Moslem quarter, between the Damascus and St. Stephen's Gates. It is a remarkable evidence of the decrease in Moslem fanaticism, that single ladies are permitted to live quietly in the heart of the Moslem quarter, without any man-servant or other protector. And even during the present excitement about the war with Russia, no insult has been offered even in the most crowded bazaars to any person; even ladies and children pass to and fro as usual;—and this at a time when the native Christians made no secret of their (very needless) dread of a Moslem rising to massacre themselves. The Moslem population is decreasing in numbers, as well as in fanaticism. It consists (within the city) of the Arab population, including, 1st, the Effendies, or ancient grandees; 2d, those who are called "Bek"—these are the gentry; and 3d, the tradespeople and artisans. All these are Arabs, and speak Arabic; but Turkish is also spoken by the Effendies. The two lower classes are honest and respectable, and, for the most part, sincere followers of Mohammed. The Effendies are luxurious, extremely corrupt, and semi-infidel. They are lax or bigoted in matters of faith and practice, as best suits the interest of the moment. They, as well as the other Moslems, are divided into the two great factions of Yemenei and Kais; and each Effendi has a number of villages in the surrounding districts of Nablous, Hebron, Gaza, Jaffa, &c., attached to his interest, by whom he, on the other hand, is regarded as a sort of protector. The government rests

---

The usual plan is to hire a house, whose size and situation are good, though dilapidated. The rent is paid for four, six, or more years in advance, on condition that the house be rebuilt or repaired, as agreed upon. Rents vary from 10*l.* per annum to 50*l.* A very few years since, they were not one-fifth of the present rate.

chiefly in the hands of Turkish officers sent annually from Constantinople, viz. Pasha and Cadi. The rank of the pashas has been recently much raised, and his excellency Hhafiz, the present pasha, has *three* horse-tails, and bears the title of Musheer (or Disposer). This latter title was never before given to a Jerusalem pasha, who was always subordinate to the Musheer of Saida, residing at Beyroot. These two officers are now both of nearly equal rank. Strangers to Jerusalem and its various interests, sometimes unable to speak or even understand Arabic, these pashas (who rarely leave the seraglio, and even the city only once or twice a-year) are much at the mercy of the council of Effendies; and thus innumerable opportunities arise for bribery, corruption, and oppression of every kind. By the time the pasha is becoming a little familiar with the names of persons and places, he is removed elsewhere, and a new stranger takes his place. The military authorities are not so often changed, but they and their soldiers are also Turks, and rarely speak any other language. The troops in Jerusalem are about 300, sometimes more. Besides these, about 200 irregular Arab cavalry are at the disposal of the pasha, and are in fact the only troops over which he has control. Their services are very various, and include the catching of thieves, the going on messages, escorting persons of rank, levying taxes from a refractory village, &c. Taxes are farmed by grasping Armenians, who take every opportunity of extorting money in the name of the government. It cannot fail to strike the most casual observer, that while the native Moslem population are diminishing in numbers and influence, the Christians, strengthened and supported from abroad, are gaining in both respects. Foreign residents and consuls of foreign nations, intimately acquainted with the history, languages, manners, and population, must needs carry weight, which the ever-changing Turkish officers could but feebly withstand, if they were able to comprehend or appreciate. This state of things is not confined to the city of Jerusalem; the Christian villages of Bethlehem,

Beit Yala, and Ramallah, are more numerously populated, clean, and prosperous than those belonging to Moslems, who scarcely keep their ground, while the others increase their lands and houses every year. The peasantry, both Moslems and Christians, are also far better acquainted with the Europeans, (who daily meet them in their walks and rides, give them medicines, encamp on their ground in summer, buy their farm-produce, and employ their services,) than they can possibly be with pashas whom they never see, and whose soldiers are but known to them as a means of enforcing payment of taxes, or the giving up of a refractory subject. The peasantry find a ready market among the Europeans and at the convents, for poultry, vegetables, fruit, corn and barley, wine, oil, straw, charcoal, wood, water, stone, lime, and other building materials; and the several thousand pounds annually expended have added so much to their buried treasures, that most of the villages are actually rich; and every year sees fresh fields cleared and sown, and more olive-trees and vines planted. Besides the daily traffic, which occupies not less than 800 camels, there is also trade carried on with Egypt in soap made in Jerusalem, and to travellers are sold great quantities of small articles manufactured in olive and Hebron oak-wood, (chiefly made by Europeans,) rosaries, boxes, mother-of-pearl shells, and various other articles made in Bethlehem, whence, moreover, several thousand pounds worth are annually exported to France, Italy, Spain, and Austria. The seaport town of Jaffa has more than doubled its number of inhabitants within seven years, and has now a population of 17,000. Seven years ago not one English merchant-ship had ever been seen there, and but few of any other nation. The first was the "John Cobbold," chartered in 1847 by the "London Society for Promoting Christianity among the Jews," to bring out the roof of Christ Church, and carpenters to put it up. Now several hundred vessels from the United States, Sweden, Norway, France, Greece, England, Italy, &c., receive and discharge cargoes. Three times per month Austrian and French steamers touch at Jaffa, for the delivery and receiving of Jerusalem mails; but there is no English steamer.[1] The port of Kaiffa has increased its trade in at least equal proportion; so has that of Sidon; while Beyroot is now a bustling mercantile town, considered to have 35,000 inhabitants.

The climate of Jerusalem is on the whole good. It would be one of the finest in the world, were common attention paid to the cleanliness of the streets and houses. During the spring and autumn months agues and fevers prevail, being engendered by the exhalations from the cisterns and rubbish accumulated in the city. But the mountain breeze rarely fails by day or night, excepting during a part of April and May, when the easterly winds are oppressive. A very little care in covering the head from the sun, avoiding too low a diet, especially undue quantities of fruit and vegetables, and in taking open air exercise, preserves the health of the Europeans; and even when they are attacked by fever or ague, the disease is easily subdued if treated without delay. Travellers are most blamably careless in all the above points, and frequently fall victims to their ignorance and folly. Many of the European residents encamp at a short distance from Jerusalem during the summer months, and are treated with the utmost respect by the peasantry, who gladly let their grounds for the pitching of their tents. Even when engaged in guerilla warfare among each other, no one case has occurred, during eight years, of incivility or annoyance to the various camps from the Arabs. On the contrary, they have been known to drive their cattle thither by night for safety. The large number of English, American, and other travellers who annually visit Jerusalem, has had a great effect upon the manners of the Arab population and the wild Bedouin. Having learnt the value of foreign gold, they respect the persons and property of those who spend so much money among them; and the visits to Petra, Jordan, and

[1] The French government and Austrian Lloyds have each a paid agent in Jerusalem.

Palestine in general, which were formerly made at the risk of life, are now a matter of business arrangement between the sheikhs, the travellers, and their consuls. How is it that persons, who are obliged to leave England in search of a milder climate, or others who prefer living abroad, do not choose the most interesting city and country in the world for their residence? Why should not young clergymen, at least, spend one year among Bible scenes, and acquiring Bible languages, before entering upon their active duties? Sixty pounds per annum would be quite enough for all expense of board and lodging, (including the keep of a horse,) for a single person, and sixty pounds more would cover the expense of the journey there and back. Even travellers, who spend a little fortune in Palestine to the enrichment of their dragomen (who sacrifice the character of their employers, and oppress and grind hotel-keepers, muleteers, &c.), know little or nothing of the country which they have passed through, under the blind guidance of blind guides. Nevertheless, the mighty tide which during three centuries impelled half the nations of Europe towards the rocky shores of Palestine—then ebbing during the temporary ascendency of Rome—is now rising annually higher. Travellers from every western nation, and 10,000 pilgrims from the East, visit the shrines of Bethlehem and Calvary; Moslems come from Arabia, Tartary, and India, and from the utmost shores of Africa, to worship at the (falsely called) Tomb of Moses. The Jewish people go to pray over the ruins of their city and temple, that the time of their deliverance may be hastened.

The deep *religious interest* in Jerusalem, which has for two thousand years been gaining strength among the nations of the earth, is becoming more intense; and high and mighty potentates study with anxious care politics, whose interest centres in Jerusalem.

It is often asked why Russia, which takes so decided a part in Oriental politics, whose interest in the sanctuaries of Jerusalem has threatened to disturb the peace of Europe, whose army annually devotes one day's pay to the support of the establishments of Jerusalem, and whose sailors may frequently be observed marching two and two, in military order, from one hallowed spot to another,—why Russia has no consul in Jerusalem? Hitherto it has been quite unnecessary that she should have any. The influence of her consul-general at Beyroot, and of her vice-consul at Jaffa, supported by the powerful Greek patriarchates and convents at Jerusalem, is quite sufficient for the protection and advancement of Russian interests. At this moment, when the dismemberment of Turkey and the occupation of Constantinople by the Russians are the engrossing themes, it has been thought by many that they have forgotten the Holy Land, or that they regard Jerusalem as a question of minor importance. Far from it. It must be remembered that the Emperor of Russia is head of the Greek Church; that "there are two almighties (autocratores)—one in heaven and one in St. Petersburg." During a period of several years, the Greek convent has been gradually extended over one-fourth of habitable Jerusalem, by the purchase of houses which have been connected with the convent, by means of arches thrown over the intervening streets. Of late, not only the houses immediately contiguous, but buildings and plots of ground in every part of the city, have been bought up by a Greek ecclesiastic, who being a native of Turkey can legally purchase. The convent cannot legally purchase land, but it is allowed in law to become possessor of property left to it by will on the death of the purchaser. The archimandrite Nikephoros has revenues so inexhaustible, that there can be no doubt as to their source. Every kind of property in the East is supposed to consist of twenty-four parts or carâts. Whether a horse, a house, a field, or a diamond, it is divisible into twenty-four carâts, and may be owned by one person or by several. Each person, in the latter case, is considered possessor of one, two, three, four, or more carâts, according to circumstances, and these descend to his heirs; so that the horse, house, field, or diamond, may at length have forty or fifty proprietors, each owning carâts, half or quarter carâts, or less, and so on; and without the consent of all, the said property cannot be let or sold. The part-proprietors have always the first choice and refusal, should the property be sold. Now, the said archimandrite is known as the purchaser of half-carâts, quarter-carâts, or whole carâts, as the case may be, of every ruined shop, house, or plot of ground, to be bought within the walls of Jerusalem; and, moreover, as possessor of immense tracts without the walls of the city, as far as Bethlehem, and in other parts of Palestine.

Even the tiny plots of vegetable garden belonging to the village of Siloam own the same person as possessor of carâts, or half-carâts. Until very recently, no part of these great possessions was cultivated; but within the last five years, many thousand mulberry and olive-trees have been planted in the neighbourhood of Jerusalem; the most unpromising hills, apparently mere masses of rock, have been cleared with the aid of gunpowder, the rich soil exposed, walls built, terraces formed, vines planted, and small annual crops raised beween the trees. Silk factories and houses are being built. At present public roads, twenty feet wide, are being made and walled in across the hills and valleys, between the Convent of the Cross and Jerusalem, a distance of twenty minutes, in order to prevent passengers from trespassing upon the plantations in progress. Gradually one piece after another is fenced in, and already the rides around Jerusalem are much interfered with by the boundary-walls, while the rich verdure is a beautiful addition to the hitherto barren landscape. Large numbers of the Moslem and Christian Arab peasantry are employed in building, ploughing, and planting; and they commonly, while calling down blessings on the Greek Convent, term the Patriarch "Aboo Dahab," (the Father of Gold.) The corrupt Effendies are also well acquainted with the various Russian coins, which are very common in the markets of Jerusalem.

Thus, while diplomacy is exercised by the various European

powers,—while able ministers are arranging the Eastern question, and studying the ancient limits of the sanctuaries, title-deeds are being accumulated in the Greek Convent, which the shock of war itself will not be able to invalidate, and which must indisputably confirm the right of the Russo-Greek purchasers to their possessions in Jerusalem and Palestine.

These are some of the effects of the *religious interest* felt for Jerusalem. Thirteen years ago, destitute and barbarous, with a plague-stricken and decreasing population, dead to trade, politics, or enterprise of any kind, Jerusalem was still the Holy City. Turkish pashas have since been sent "to protect the interests of the Christians." England and Prussia have founded their Protestant bishopric; Austria defends the Roman Catholic institutions; France appears as "Protector of Christianity in the East;" and the Emperor of the Russias is head of the most ancient Gentile Church in Jerusalem, Asia, or the world; while around the holy place, whence the glory has departed, still lingers the Jewish people—their sole support that quenchless faith in the promises of God, which eighteen centuries of suffering have not been able to diminish or to abate. How often it is said, in these *enlightened* times, that politics have nothing to do with religion! and yet it has ever been found that the fiercest and most intense political struggles are those which arise out of religious questions. The desolating wars of the Greek empire, the Crusades, and the Reformation, may serve to warn us what convulsions may yet shake the nations, when the tide of *politico-religious interest* in Jerusalem has burst the barriers which still feebly oppose its rising floods.[1]

The Diocesan School was established by his Lordship the Bishop, and opened Nov. 10, 1847. It contains at present

[1] To this statement it may be desirable to add a few particulars. A scheme for the foundation of a College at Jerusalem has even been set on foot, though at present it is quite in its infancy. The Principal is W. Beamont, Fellow of the University of Cambridge.

near forty boys and twenty-eight girls, of all classes and religions; some children of each sex are boarded in the Prussian Hospice. The instruction is based upon Protestant Christianity, and the parents of the children are all aware that no compromise is made in favour of any; but that, with quiet regularity, the New Testament is read, and Christian principle inculcated as a matter of daily routine. Yet Jewish children of the rabbinical families, and some Moslems of both sexes, are to be found there. A friend's note-book observes,—" The boys are taught English, Hebrew, and Arabic. I heard them go through a lesson in natural history, and read part of the 24th chapter of St. Luke: the answers were tolerably satisfactory. Some of the class were Jewish proselytes. The school appears to be well conducted, and to be doing good."

The Industrial Plantation, for employment of poor Jews in agriculture, consists of a piece of land on a rising ground, at about half-an-hour's walk northwards from the city. The purchase has been made by subscriptions from benevolent persons in England, India, and the United States; the property is committed to trustees in Jerusalem. The necessity for this undertaking arises from the extreme poverty of the Jewish people in this city, and the unhealthiness of their places of abode, which latter circumstance renders employment of this character more conducive to health than any that could be provided within the walls.

The plot of land was partially planted in the last spring with olive-trees and mulberries: these will be added to, and vines planted there in the coming winter. Walls have been built around, and ancient cisterns cleared out: these last, however, require repairing.

Another valuable institution is the House of Industry, for the training of Jewish converts to Christianity in useful trades, in combination with religious instruction. This is a necessary accompaniment to a mission for the conversion of the Jews; as those who embrace Christianity are thereby deprived of employment among their brethren, and thrown in great measure upon the Society for support. The trades, adopted almost exclusively, are those of carpentering and turning; the objects manufactured are those most in request by travellers, for distribution, on their return home, as remembrances of Jerusalem.

Next upon the list is the Female School of Industry, conducted by Miss Cooper with assistants, for instruction of Jewesses in useful needlework, and continuing them in employment when instructed. This institution, founded in 1848, independent of any society, has been productive of excellent results. Previous to its existence, the ignorance of the Jewish women in Jerusalem in useful domestic needlework was truly deplorable. The average attendance is fifty.

One of the most beneficial results arising from the English mission is the establishment of an hospital for Jewish and other patients, for which unhappily there was but too much occasion at Jerusalem, from the poverty of this people, their wretched diet, and their filthy, unwholesome habitations. Through the benevolence of Sir Moses Montefiore, a medical man was indeed sent out to mitigate the sufferings of his brethren; but still there is but too wide a field for the operations of the English hospital. The building is healthily situated (see view on title-page) on the brow of Mount Zion, and adjacent to it is the house of Dr. Macgowan, the principal medical officer, and many years a resident in the city, whose management of the hospital is universally a subject of praise. I was conducted over the establishment by an old acquaintance, whom I had first known many years before as a Jewish convert at Damascus, and who has ever since maintained an undeviating consistency of conduct, which testified to the sincerity of his convictions. The general superintendence of the establishment has been committed to his care, and the cleanliness and good order that reign throughout testify to the excellence of his stewardship.

The first steps towards the establishment of this valuable

institution was the sending out, in 1838, a medical missionary, Mr. Gerstmann, who, being himself a converted Jew, was certain to sympathise with the distressed condition of his countrymen. In spite of threats of excommunication put forth by the rabbis on all who should hold communication with the missionaries, the messenger of healing was gladly welcomed to the abodes of poverty and disease. The result of his visits was the discovery of a mass of filth, misery, and destitution, which urgently stimulated the benevolent missionaries to undertake an effectual measure of relief. " Our plan," wrote Mr. Nicolayson, " is to form something that may grow into a hospital. Be not alarmed at the name ' Hospital ;' we are not going to erect a palace like the hospitals in London. Our idea is this: if we receive one pound only, we will spend this in procuring a little broth and other such necessaries for those poor Jews and Jewesses who are recovering, and for want of it must relapse into more hopeless misery and suffering. If we receive 5l., or 10l., or 15l., we will do the same on a proportionably extended scale. If we receive 20l. or more, (as we certainly trust the time will come when we shall,) we can then take a clean and airy room, and receive the most destitute and helpless into it. One great cause of the shocking diseases and accumulated wretchedness among Jews here, is the manner in which they are compelled to crowd and herd together; three or four families in one little dark, damp, and dirty room!" The absolute necessity of some such measure to give effect to the missionary labours, and the direct manner in which it would bring those relieved under the influence and instruction of the mission, besides the moral effect it would produce on Jews, Christians, and Moslems, were also pleaded in behalf of the undertaking; nor was the appeal in vain. Funds were raised —Mr. Gerstmann continued his labours—a dispensary was established — and Mr. Bergheim, a believing Israelite, assisted in giving out the medicines. The arrival in 1842 of Dr. Macgowan, the able physician appointed by the " London Society for Promoting Christianity among the Jews," gave a still further impulse to the work. His report painfully exposed the condition of the poorer class of Jews. "Their dwellings," he says, "are in dark vaulted caves, the roof dripping with damp from above, and the bare earth beneath, and often without door or window to keep out the wind and rain. It is in these dark and dismal abodes that the descendant of God's chosen people drags out a miserable existence, and presents a striking fulfilment of that utter desolation which has fallen on his city and nation. The necessaries of life, which are already too scanty in health, are miserably deficient in sickness. The want of attendance, of cleanliness, of suitable nourishment, and of ordinary precautions, is quite appalling. The absence of these destroys more lives than the disease itself." The necessity for establishing an hospital was warmly urged by the doctor, and generally responded to by the Society. A suitable house was soon found and fitted up. It was opened on the 12th Dec. 1844, and it has ever since been fully occupied. The benefit thus conferred upon the poor Jews has been incalculable, and cannot but have largely added to the ultimate success of the mission.

I was enabled to form some idea of the necessity and value of such an institution on the morning when I visited it. There were about fifty applicants for out-door relief then crowding the dispensary, whose pallid, sunken faces spoke painfully of disease and destitution; low fever, most probably engendered by unhealthy abodes and poor diet, seemed to be the predominant complaint.

The maintenance of this establishment is one of the largest items in the Society's expenditure, amounting, in the year 1853, to the sum of 1,230*l*. 3*s*. The number of patients admitted into the wards during the year was 414, while 7,364 others have, as out-door patients, enjoyed the benefits connected with this valuable institution.

Besides this admirable institution, there is another founded by the King of Prussia, called the Evangelical Hospice. The building is small but handsome, not far from the English Church, consisting of a hospital, with accommodation for learned travellers duly recommended; and to this a noble library is to be attached.

The medical part of this establishment is conducted by the Prussian deaconesses, under the professional advice of Dr. Macgowan, of the Jewish Society's hospital. Upwards of eighty patients, without distinction of nation or creed, were received there during the year 1852-3.

The spiritual care is that of Pastor F. Valentiner, of the German Evangelical community.

The deaconesses form a branch of the central establishment at Kaiserswerth, near the Rhine. Their number is five, and they are attached principally to the service of the Hospice. These are not under vows, like the Lazarist Sisters of Charity, but have signed a paper of indenture, or subscription to the regulations of the general association. Of this institution is added a further notice by a friend:—" If the term pretty be applicable to a hospital, the greatest gem which I ever saw in that way is the establishment of the King of Prussia, over which the Lutheran Sisters of Charity preside. The institution has three branches: 1st, an orphan house, where motherless girls are received and educated by the four sisters, in German and needlework, during the afternoon of each day. In the morning they go to the Diocesan School. One poor Abyssinian slave has been adopted by the Sisters, after purchase from her master. The children are of every persuasion, Christians, Mahometans, &c., and their number nine or ten. There are besides, 2dly, an infirmary; and 3dly, a hospice. From the terrace is a pleasant view over the city, and the cultivation of flowers bears witness to the good taste of the sisterhood. The two Sisters whom I saw made a very favourable impression upon me; they speak English, and seem thoroughly benevolent, and desirous to discharge their office from the heart."

The quiet perseverance of the noble-minded women who have devoted themselves to this sphere of labour, cannot but prove a most valuable auxiliary to the mission. Nothing is more needful than to raise the tone of female character in the East, if Christianity and civilization are to obtain a wider influence. In 1853, fifty Jewesses were under the care of Miss Cooper and her assistant Miss Railton. These ladies were then learning the Judeo-Spanish dialect, in order to read to and converse with their charge. The women were flattered by this acquisition of their language, and began to listen with pleasure and interest to the instructions of the ladies, and the reading of the Holy Scriptures.

In addition to the "London Jewish Society," must not be omitted the "Church Missionary Society," conducted by C. Sandreezki, Esq. The religious services are at present conducted in the Diocesan School-room, except on Sacrament Sundays, when the native Christians, who have placed themselves under the English episcopate, assemble at an early hour for the usual order of communion service and a sermon, both in the Arabic language. They communicate at the table with the general congregation, after the English service.

From this detailed account of the recent improvements in the social condition of the city, I must now turn to other topics. In company with Mr. Rogers, at that time the British Vice-Consul, I paid a visit to the Armenian Convent, to see the new palace of the Patriarch, then recently finished, and said to contain the most spacious and splendid apartments in Jerusalem. The site of this extensive and wealthy establishment is undoubtedly the pleasantest in the city, as its inmates may be considered the aristocracy of the monkish fraternity, and, as observed in the "Walks," is probably not far from the beautiful palace gardens of Herod. Opposite to the façade of the building is a wall enclosing the gardens, which, though exhibiting no taste, display some magnificent vegetation, altogether unlike anything else either within or without the walls.

The convent is dedicated to St. James, the first bishop of Jerusalem, the spot of whose martyrdom is pointed out in the church.

The convent is said to have been founded by Abgarus, who supported poor persons there for seven years; and as the convent was enriched, buildings were erected on the spots marked out by him, till it has swelled into the dimensions of a small town, surrounded by a wall of its own.

The great wealth obtained by the influx of pilgrims may have originated the established rule that every successive Patriarch shall add some new building to the convent. Passing through some of the older parts of the edifice, we reached the new apartments, which are built across the roadway in front of the convent, thus connecting it with the garden on the opposite side. They are certainly, for Jerusalem, both spacious and handsome, in the modern Italian style in fashion at Constantinople. We were introduced to the Patriarch by his interpreter; and after complimenting him upon the splendour of his new abode, were regaled by him with coffee and sweetmeats. The conversation, which passed through the medium of an interpreter, turned chiefly on the Eastern question, in the solution of which he seems to be greatly interested. It may be remarked that, of all the religious bodies in Jerusalem, the Armenians have looked upon the English episcopate influence with the most friendly, or, perhaps more correctly, with the least jealous eye.

Connected with this extensive and wealthy convent, is a Clerical Seminary already in existence, but the plan of which will not be fully carried out till the new buildings are completed. It is intended to educate twenty youths during a course of seven years, for ecclesiastics, at the end of which period they may select the country in which to reside, or they may take canonical vows if they prefer to do so. The edifice for this purpose is being prepared on a noble scale within the precincts of the great convent.

There is also a very handsome printing-press, which has been at work for several years. The works issued comprise some of modern times that are highly esteemed among them; a popular Commentary on Scripture, besides the usual standard publications of Eastern Churches, the Psalms, Gospels, &c. This establishment is to be removed to the ground-floor of the Clerical Seminary.

There is a daily distribution at the convent gate of food to the poor; but in this community the poor members are but few. And the Abyssinian Convent is fed daily with broth or gruel from this establishment, in return for certain lands, said to have been appropriated by the Armenians, but of which the title-deeds were buried, after a plague in the city, about twenty years ago.

I walked out one evening to examine that part of Mount Zion now without the walls, though there can be no doubt it must have been formerly included within them. There is indeed a tradition, that the best Saracenic builder was put to death for the blunder of not enclosing all the level ground on the hill-top, —thus leaving it as a vantage-ground for a besieging army. Dr. Robinson, however, supposes it to take the same line as in the city built by Adrian. It was on this open spot that Raymond, Count of Toulouse, encamped his detachment of the Crusaders, during the celebrated siege by Godfrey of Bouillon.

There is little difficulty in tracing the line of the ancient first wall at this particular point. It appears to have followed the brink of the hill from north to south, bending round just above the new English burial-ground, though its further course towards the Temple is matter of great uncertainty; some carrying it along the ridge at the top, and excluding the fountain of Siloam, while others run it below, so as to include it. The open space on the hill-top is partly occupied by two buildings—the traditionary Tomb of David, and an Armenian building, said to enclose the house of Caiaphas, and partly by different Christian cemeteries. This group is well represented in a sketch obligingly furnished by Miss Barclay.

The American cemetery appears in the centre of the sketch, enclosed within a wall. This plot of ground was purchased by the missionaries, in consequence of the growing intolerance of the Greek Christians, which forbade any further interments of Protestants in their burial-ground. Two members of the Mission,

Mrs. Thomson and Dr. Dodge, had died in Jerusalem; and, as Dr. Robinson informs us, " a grave was sought and obtained for the former without difficulty in their cemetery. In the case of the latter, the same permission was granted, and a grave dug; but, as they were about to proceed to the burial, word was brought that the permission had been recalled, and the grave filled up. On a strong representation of the case to the heads of the Greek Convent, the burial was allowed to take place, with the express understanding that a like permission would never more be given. In consequence, the missionaries purchased this little spot on Mount Zion." It has since been enclosed within a solid wall of stone.

Nearer to the city wall is the Armenian, and also the Greek and Latin cemeteries. These are unenclosed, and the monuments for the most part are mere white slabs, placed lengthwise over the grave. In the cemetery of the Latins was interred a young American, who died in their convent in 1830, and whose conversion from the "errors of Luther and Calvin" is pompously inscribed upon his monument by the monks. Not far off, is also that of the unfortunate Costigan, who perished in consequence of his attempt to explore the Dead Sea.

Just below the brow of this funeral hill, on one of the lowest prominences of Mount Zion, is situated the new English cemetery.

The annexed view, from the opposite side of the valley, will give a good idea of its situation. In front is the end of the pool, with the wall built across the valley to dam up the water. The dry bottom of the pool serves as an excellent threshing-floor. Below are seen the abrupt cliffs of the Hill of Evil Counsel, overhanging the gloomy valley of Hinnom. On its summit are the ruins of the traditional house of Annas, the high-priest, when counsel was taken to put Jesus to death; and grouped with it appropriately enough, with the usual licence of mediæval tradition, is seen an old tree, on which Judas is said to have hung himself. We found the gate open, and the men at work upon some buildings connected with the ground, which has not been long laid out.

On the eastern side, the burial-ground is enclosed by a ridge of rocks, evidently scarped, most probably forming, as has been conjectured, the foundation of the old or first wall by which Mount Zion was enclosed; while a little below runs the aqueduct conveying the water from Solomon's Pool into the city.

The British government made a liberal contribution towards the purchase of the ground in 1848, to which the bishop having added other funds, the property was vested in the episcopate, and part of the ground that was purchased is separated from the rest for other purposes.

The English and Prussian Protestant burials, previous to 1848, had taken place in a piece of ground near the Mamilla Turkish cemetery; but the Moslems had always been dissatisfied with it, and a wall of enclosure would not have been allowed. The bodies were therefore removed to the new ground, on the 26th and 27th of July of that year.

The principal persons interred are—

    1. Bishop Alexander, deceased November 23, 1845.
    2. R. Bateson, Esq. M.P. deceased December 26, 1843.
    3. Dr. Schultz, Prussian Consul, deceased October 22, 1851.

We returned to the hill-top, and entering into the curious and irregular jumble of buildings, which in the Saracenic architecture of the Moslems has been grafted upon the original gothic of the monks, we were shown up a flight of stairs to the Cænaculum, or "upper room," where Christ ate the passover with his disciples; another clumsy legend, though of great antiquity, which has not the semblance of verisimilitude—the arches that support the chamber being pointed, and evidently of Christian origin. A Church appears to have been erected here, in very early times, and was said to contain the column to which Christ was fastened before being scourged. The adjacent buildings were, formerly, the Latin or Franciscan convent, till the middle of the fifteenth century, when, being expelled thence by the Moslems, the fathers removed to their present abode within the city.

Arculf, A.D. 700, here saw a square church which included the Cœnaculum—the place where the Holy Ghost descended upon the apostles; the marble column to which our Lord was bound when he was scourged; and the spot where the Virgin Mary died. Here also was shown the site of the martyrdom of St. Stephen. Sœwulf, four centuries later, also alludes to this place as having escaped destruction by the pagans. He speaks of the marble table which served for the Lord's supper. He says also, "Under the wall of the city, outside, on the declivity of Mount Zion, is the Church of St. Peter, which is called the Gallican, where, after having denied his Lord, he hid himself in a very deep crypt, as may still be seen there, and there wept bitterly for his offence." Mandeville also alludes to all these localities.

Between this mass of buildings and the Zion Gate is also a building surrounded by an irregular wall, a dependency upon the great Armenian Convent just within the gate. This, too, is rich in legendary localities and objects, equally authentic with the preceding. It is called the House of Caiaphas, the high-priest, whither our Lord was conducted for judgment. Maundrell's account of it is as good as any. "Here, under the altar, they tell us is deposited that very stone which was laid to secure the door of our Saviour's sepulchre; but the Armenians, not many years since, stole it from thence by a stratagem, and conveyed it to this place. The stone is two yards and a quarter long, high one yard, and broad as much. It is plastered all over, except in five or six little places, where it is left bare to receive the immediate kisses and other devotions of pilgrims. Here is likewise shown a little cell, said to have been our Lord's prison till the morning when he was carried from hence before Pilate; and also the place where Peter was frightened into a denial of his Master."

The Turkish name of the building is *Neby Daood*, or Sanctuary of the Sepulchre of David. The institution is richly endowed, on condition of exercising hospitality to strangers. The mass of buildings has been agglomerated in process of time, as the family of the original guardian has increased to its present very large number.

Considerable mystery hangs over the tomb of the poet king. St. Peter, addressing the Jews, thus speaks: "his sepulchre is with us unto this day." The treasures contained in the royal mausoleum had previously led to two sacrilegious attempts to rifle it,—first, by the high-priest Hyrcanus, and second, by Herod the Great. Josephus tells a marvellous story about the latter breaking in by night, and being defeated of his purpose by the sudden bursting out of flames, as were the Jews who attempted to rebuild the temple under Julian. A story, no less extraordinary, is told of it by Benjamin of Tudela, who visited Jerusalem during its occupation by the Crusaders:—

"On Mount Zion are the sepulchres of the house of David, and those of the kings who reigned after him. In consequence of the following circumstance, however, this place is at present hardly to be recognised. Fifteen years ago, one of the walls of the place of worship fell down, and the Patriarch ordered the priest to repair it. He ordered stones to be taken from the original wall of Zion for that purpose; and twenty workmen were hired at stated wages, who broke stones from the very foundations of the walls of Zion. Two of these labourers, who were intimate friends, upon a certain day treated one another, and repaired to their work after their friendly meal. The overseer accused them of dilatoriness, but they answered that they would still perform their day's work, and would employ thereupon the time while their fellow-labourers were at meals. They then continued to break out stones, until happening to meet with one which formed the mouth of a cavern, they agreed to enter it in search of treasure; and they proceeded until they reached a large hall supported by pillars of marble, encrusted with gold and silver, and before which stood a table with a golden sceptre and crown. This was the Sepulchre of David, king of Israel; to the left of which they saw that of Solomon in a similar state; and so on, the sepulchres of the kings of Judah who were buried there. They further saw chests locked up, the contents of which nobody knew, and were on the point of entering the hall, when a blast of wind, like a storm, issued forth of the mouth of the cavern so strong, that it threw them almost lifeless to the ground. There they lay till evening, when another wind rushed forth, from which they heard a voice like that of a man calling aloud, 'Get up, and go forth from this place.' The men rushed out full of fear, and proceeded to the Patriarch to report what had happened to them. This ecclesiastic summoned into his presence R. Abraham el Constantini, a pious ascetic, one of the mourners of the fate of Jerusalem, and caused the two labourers to repeat what they had previously repeated. R. Abraham thereupon informed the Patriarch that they had discovered the sepulchres of the house of David and of the kings of Judah. The following morning the labourers were sent for again, but they were found stretched upon their beds and full of fear; they declared they would not attempt to go again to the cave, as it was not God's will to discover it to any one. The Patriarch ordered the place to be walled up, so as to hide it effectually from everybody to the present day. The above-mentioned R. Abraham told me all this."

Making liberal allowance for the credulity of the times, it is far from improbable that future excavations may throw some light upon this marvellous tale.

AN EVENING ON MOUNT ZION.

I do not know that I ever received a deeper impression of the fallen condition of Zion than on one occasion when I repaired thither to survey from its brow the opposite south-west angle of the Haram wall, respecting which my curiosity had been excited by certain statements in the last edition of Mr. Williams' "Holy City." The sun was almost setting when I passed beneath the splendid apartments of the Armenian Patriarch; and leaving on the right the Zion Gate and the huts of the wretched lepers, followed the inner line of the wall as nearly as I was able, toward the point I was desirous of reaching. The path, deep in dust, lay through thickets of the prickly pear, with which the slope of Zion is here covered, and heaps of filthy rags and rubbish, among which were crouching a number of the wretched curs, which act as a sort of scavengers to the city. A few hovels, the outskirts of the Jewish quarter, were on my left; and a few of their straggling tenants, who carried privation and sickliness in their pallid countenances, passed me occasionally with listless and feeble footstep. The savage clamour of the dogs, as they rose from their lurking-places, and howled from a distance at the apparition of a passing Frank, added to the sensation of dreariness and melancholy produced by the entire scene.

At length I reached the abrupt edge of the cliffs which command the opposite angle of the temple. It was where the last defenders of Jerusalem took refuge after the destruction of the city by Titus, overlooking the smoking and blood-stained ruins of the Temple; from which, according to Josephus, they were separated only by the bridge, across which Titus harangued them, with a view to induce them to surrender. And though the revolutions of centuries have passed over the spot—though the Temple and its courts have disappeared, and the Saracens and the Crusaders have occupied its site with other edifices—enough remains to identify all the prominent positions, and to bring back to the mind's eye the vanished splendour of Jerusalem, and the last scenes of her terrible overthrow.

But the annexed view will speak more eloquently than words of these mutations. We are standing on the brow of Zion, upon heaps of rubbish, the ruins of her palaces and towers overgrown with thickets of prickly pear, which extend almost to the opposite ruined wall of the Temple. The intervening valley of the Tyropeon thus occupied, was formerly, there can be no doubt, deeper than at the present day, and probably one of the main thoroughfares of the city. Casting our eyes across it, the first object that arrests attention is the angle of the enclosure, with its courses of massive ancient masonry extending along its southern and western faces, and though partly concealed by a pile of modern houses, appearing again on the latter side at the "Jews' Wailing Place," forming, there can be no doubt, part of a line extending along the whole enclosure. Starting prominently from this masonry, near the angle, is part of a ruined arch, the appearance of which is, architecturally speaking, quite inexplicable, unless we suppose it to have formed part of a bridge extending across the valley, and forming a communication with the opposite heights of Zion; and such a bridge we know to have existed, from various passages in Josephus.

The southern wall of the enclosure displays the same massive masonry, as far as the point where it is concealed by some Saracenic buildings, which terminate the modern city wall at its junction with that of the "Haram;" and again beyond that point at intervals to the distant south-east angle, where there is again a most remarkable display of it. An inspection of the drawing will show that all the courses of stones above these lowest and massive ones, are of smaller character, and very much mixed in style, being evidently the work of later builders, who have piled up their inferior masonry on the majestic ruins of the original wall.

Conspicuous above the centre of the southern wall, is the Mosque el Aksa, branching from which, as far as the south-west corner, is the Mosque of Abu Bekr, and along the western wall that of the Mogrebins, from which arises a minaret. The whole of this end of the enclosure is sustained on arches, through which a gateway, two hundred feet long, the external entrance to which is enclosed, runs up on a slope to the level of the platform above.

In the distance appears the Mosque of Omar, and seen across the deep intervening valley of Jehoshaphat, the summit of the Mount of Olives, with the Mosque of the Ascension, the Chapel of the Prediction, and an Arab tower, from which was taken our panoramic view of the city. At the bend of the city wall, near the foreground, appears the modern Dung Gate, now shut up.

The principal object in seeking this spot, was to examine a statement put forth with no small parade of superior accuracy by Mr. Williams, to the effect, that in his new map of the city, drawn up after a survey by the Royal Engineers, this south-west line of the Temple enclosure was for the first time correctly represented. For while acknowledging that Mr. Catherwood's survey of the interior of the Haram is by far the most complete that has been attempted, he observes that " his proceedings were brought to an abrupt close by the approach of Ibrahim Pasha; and a comparison of his plan with that of the Officers will show, that although he succeeded in laying down minute architectural plans of the edifices which occupy the area, his general survey of that area must have been left incomplete; for it is impossible to doubt the exactness of the military survey, and the discrepancies between the two are in some instances very great." Nor is it less strange that not only Dr. Robinson and the American missionaries, but the rest of the modern travellers, had most unaccountably contrived to overlook this point. Mr. Williams observes, with no small pride, "The publication of the first accurate plan of the Holy City may justly be regarded as an era in the literature of the subject; and I have spared no pains to make the Companion worthy of the work which it is designed to illustrate." And no one can doubt that he has been perfectly successful in so doing. The discrepancy between Mr. Catherwood's and the Royal Engineers' is this, that the former represents the line of the old wall from the south-west corner to the "Jews' Wailing Place," and so further on, as perfectly straight

and continuous, whereas the latter lay down an angle in it of several feet, as here illustrated.

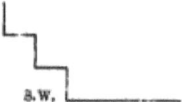

This alteration is confidently adopted by Mr. Williams; nor does he, in his usual style, hesitate to declare that this exactness of the Ordnance, " in respect to the disputed points," is fully borne out by the most faithful drawings of those artists who have of late years sketched the area from buildings or elevations in its vicinity. We observe in a note: " An inspection of Lady Louisa Tenison's and Mr. Tipping's views of the west wall of the Haram, from the opposite brow of Zion (the same spot from which my own annexed view was drawn), and of M. Girault de Prangey's beautiful and very accurate view of the Haram, taken from the roof of the Seraiyeh, will justify this remark." This is an extraordinary specimen of the way in which this writer " à tort et à travers," presses others into his service when it happens to suit his purpose. What! a view taken from the roof of the Governor's house, at the northern end of the Haram, and representing only its interior, illustrate a disputed point, (not thence even visible) at the exterior extremity of the southern! A view of St. Peter's at Rome would, certes, be equally to the purpose. Lady Louisa Tenison's view has not fallen under my observation; but that of Mr. Tipping is before me as I write, and it has absolutely no bearing whatever upon the disputed question.

But, were it not totally unfounded, it is but a poor compliment to the superior accuracy of these artists, that they confirm his new and corrected plan; for, alas, those very corrections turn out themselves to be incorrect.

After the very confident assertions of Mr. Williams, I was really surprised to perceive, at the very first glance from the opposite brow of Zion, that the accuracy of Mr. Catherwood's plan was perfectly unquestionable; and could only assign as the cause of this strange mistake of the Engineers, the very one by which Mr. Williams supposes Mr. Catherwood himself to have been deceived. " There is a gate just south of the 'Jews' Wailing Place' which gives access to the Mosque enclosure, but is chiefly used by the family of Abu Se' ud Effendi, the principal entrance to whose house is just within the gate, while there is a back entrance a little to the north of the ruined arch. This house was obviously the main cause of embarrassment; the fact being that it does form an angle of the western wall of the Haram, as is also represented in Mr. Catherwood's plan, and that the wall, as thus broken, does not resume the same direct line as he imagined, but is continued in a line many feet to the west. This enables us to reconcile the discrepancies between his plan and the Officers' survey." And this it undoubtedly does, though in the opposite sense to what Mr. Williams supposes. Next day I repaired to the spot, to satisfy myself that the work was straight —a conviction fully confirmed by the most accurate measurements taken by parties living close to the spot, and never doubted, I believe, by any one in the city, until the publication of Mr. Williams's remarks.

But the real cause of this writer's giving such prominence to this imaginary correction, is mainly the support it is supposed to contribute to a theory probably no less imaginary. According to his view, the whole of this portion of the wall formed no part of the Temple, and the vaults within were built by Justinian to support his celebrated Church of St. Mary; and, consequently, the fragment supposed to be that of the bridge to Zion is only a portion of these substructions—the real bridge being, in fact, the causeway to the north of it, across which the street of David leads down to the entrance of the Haram. With characteristic modesty and candour he observes, " I apprehend, then, that *none but such as have prejudged the question* will hesitate to admit that the claims of the causeway, to be regarded as the bridge, are superior to those of the arch; and it is a satisfaction to find that the argument, as above stated, approved itself to archæologists, before the discovery of *another fact* which must determine the point *beyond all doubt;* at least as regards the ruined arch; for it now appears that this fragment is not on the same line with the remainder of the west wall of the Haram, but that there are two distinct breaks in the continuity of that line towards its southern part, one immediately south of the causeway, the other south of the 'Jews' Wailing Place.'" And then, in a note, he adds, "This will show the value of Dr. Robinson's remark on the relative distance between the brow of Zion and the opposite end of the valley, at the arch and at the causeway." As, however, the "Jews' Wailing Place" is an obstacle in the way of Mr. Williams's theory, that the Temple wall must have ended a little to the north of it, he is so kind as to endeavour, for the sake of the poor Jews, to "bring the Wailing Place within the boundary of the Temple;" not, however, without a hint that they may after all be mistaken as to the great antiquity of these stones. In order to effect this benevolent purpose, he assigns the wall as the western termination of the Royal Porch of Herod, erected probably without the bounds of the ancient Temple, (!) and finally concludes : "Thus will a satisfactory account be given of both the angles that break the continuity of the western wall; for that nearest the causeway will mark the limit of the old area before its extension by Herod the Great, and the angle south of the Wailing Place will determine the south wall of the Royal Cloister, while all south of this will belong to the Church and Hospitals of Justinian, built in great measure on an artificial foundation," &c. And it must be admitted, that the account is just as satisfactory as the angles to which it relates are authentic.

A ramble through the Jewish quarter will convince the traveller, that whatever improvement may have taken place among the Franks, or in the Armenian Convent, little, if any, has been effected among the squalid habitations of the Jews upon Mount Zion; and their quarter is still the foulest and the most unhealthy in the city.

When the author first visited Jerusalem, the English Mission had not fairly taken root. It was then observed that of all places upon earth, this city seemed the most unpromising to attack Judaism, where every surrounding object tended so strongly to fortify its traditions, and where the disputes among Christians presented a standing argument against the truth and influence of their religion. It is difficult to say how far the assiduous labours of the missionaries have been attended with success; whether the few converts they have made, and the influence they have established, are to be referred chiefly to interested considerations; or whether, on the other hand, they may be looked upon as really genuine and hopeful evidences that the prejudices of this people are getting undermined, and that their conversion to Christianity is not so improbable as might at first sight appear. So far as the reports of the missionaries are concerned, we might be led to suppose the latter was the case; but it must be remembered that such reports, however honest, are liable to be coloured unconsciously by the hopes and wishes of the writers.

Any symptom, it must be confessed, is better than a state of stagnant indifference; and we cannot, therefore, be surprised that the bishop should say in his report, (whatever some may think of such language,) that "what encourages him most is, that there is a considerable stir amongst the Jews, with much hatred against some of the proselytes, which is generally a sign that there is some good being done among them." It is admitted, that some of these proselytes are far from creditable acquisitions; and experience has convinced the missionaries, that they "must be prepared to see some of them go back to the Jews and to their bad habits."

One thing that tends to withhold any Jews who might feel

disposed to embrace Christianity from making an open confession, is the almost despotic power exercised over them by the rabbis. As the law stands at present (1853) should a Jew embrace Christianity, he must be prepared to separate from his wife and children, unless the question, which has been referred to Constantinople, is decided in his favour. Another obstacle is the loss of employment or alms among his brethren, and his being thrown entirely upon the missionaries for the means of support. It requires no small faith and energy to meet such difficulties as these for conscience' sake. And we are assured that "notwithstanding these things, a spirit of inquiry is spreading among the Jews, and that there are many secret believers, who are only kept back from an open confession of their faith through the painful circumstances in which such a confession would involve them." If this is really the case, it cannot be doubted, that when the civil and religious liberties of Christians and Jews are eventually established by the Great Powers upon a firm basis, these secret converts will openly declare themselves.

The following account of the Jews in Jerusalem has been furnished me upon the best authority. There are—

1. Sephardim, or Rayah Jews of the Spanish race, driven out of Spain in 1497 by Ferdinand and Isabella, who then formed settlements throughout Barbary and the Levant.

They speak Spanish, in various shades of admixture with Greek and Turkish; but the high families speak a good dialect, and preserve in it many antique words no longer used in Spain.

They are very careful of their genealogies.

This community consists of nearly 6,000 souls, and is not subdivided into minor sects.

Under the Turkish government, they have their own rabbinical laws, without distinction into civil and ecclesiastical.

The Chief Rabbi is popularly called the *Chacham Bashi* in Turkish; but his Hebrew title is one of peculiar dignity,— הראשון בציון " the first in Zion."

His official dragoman has a seat in the Mejlis, or Pasha's Council, as well as the dragoman of each of the Christian convents.

Under the chief are seven leading rabbis, forming his council. These are in permanent office; but each of these has a minor council of two or three rabbis as assistant-judges or assessors, who are changed every three months.

The financial affairs of the community are administered by its own officers; but its debt is enormous, with interest of the obligations paid to Moslems and the convents at an excessively high rate; and great dissatisfaction exists among the laity with respect to that administration.

The Sephardim synagogues are four in number. One of them, rebuilt a few years ago by the Minhkas family, from the desolations of ages, is believed to have been a synagogue in the time of the second Temple.

The only alms for the poor consist in what the wardens obtain by going round to the houses of the non-paupers, on each Friday morning; it is generally bestowed in loaves of bread.

About the beginning of 1853, the community was obliged to stop all other kind of relief.

2. Ashkenazim, or Jews of German, Polish, and Russian origin. These are not quite so numerous as the Sephardim, but may amount to 5,000.

These were only readmitted to Palestine, as a body, about fifty years ago. Being European foreigners, they came in under the wing of the Sephardim subjects, who recognised them as Israelites in dealing with Turkish authorities; but, in return, exacted certain conditions, which are now felt to be oppressive in proportion as the Ashkenazim rise to importance in the country.

These are divided into three sects: (1) Perushim, (2) Chasidim, (3) Hhabàdnik. The first has two synagogues, the others one each, with its own rabbis, treasurers, wardens, &c.

THE ASHKENAZIM COMMUNITY.

The chief judge among the Ashkenazim is R. Yeshaiah, but the only Hebrew authority recognised by the Turkish government is the *Chacham Bashi* of the Sephardim. The Ashkenazim being foreigners, are not amenable to Turkish law, but are under the jurisdiction of their respective consuls.

The Ashkenazim, as well as Sephardim, have collections of money sent to them from all nations in the world; for at the door of each synagogue is a box, with the word *Jerusalem* upon it. These sums arriving here, are distributed also among the other holy cities. The money is transmitted generally by means of messengers, sent from Jerusalem on purpose, who contract to go and return, &c. for a certain per-centage on the amount of the collections,—a clumsy but ancient practice. From Austria, however, the collections are now transmitted through Constantinople banks. Large sums arrive every year, but the number to share in its distribution is so great, that much poverty exists among them.

Still the Ashkenazim community has no debt; and every person—rich, poor, young, old—every person belonging to it, and of whatever subdivided sect, receives three magyars of fifty-five piastres each, annually, because he lives in Jerusalem. Another source of income is found in the houses of religious study, called Beth-ha-Midrash, where a fixed number of men are employed in rotation every night to read the Law or commentators: these receive ten piastres for each occasion, or near two shillings.

It is true that but little handicraft trade is to be found in Jerusalem, but it is also true that the system of the Rabbis discourages such employment,—its efforts being directed to the sustenance of a population reading "the Law day and night," (Psal. i. 2.) This system, by its erroneous mode of practice, indirectly creates a nation of paupers depending upon them for bread.

A circumstance not generally known is, that the Jews pass

a cheap kind of coin among themselves, at a pará each, though not worth more than one-fifth of a pará. These are square bits of brass-foil, stamped with the words בקור חולים "visiting the sick," and probably originated in the distribution of alms to the needy. Other people than Jews will occasionally accept them as currency; and the practice is not confined in the East to the Holy Land.

The other holy cities of the Jews are,—1, Hebron, on account of the Patriarchs; 2, Safed; and 3, Tiberius, on account of the Talmudists.

Generally speaking, the same sects are found in each of these cities; but it is probable that the communities of Galilee (Safed, Tiberias, Shafa, Amer, and B'kéa) have been less disturbed by the revolutions of empires and centuries than that of Jerusalem.

It is well known that out of Palestine, the Jews use an exclamation annually at Passover, בשנת הבא בירושלם "Next year in Jerusalem;" but in this country, the fervent desire is expressed in Chaldee form, בארעא דישראל "Next year in the land of Israel."

It is to be observed that they do not use the term "Holy Land" in the same sense as Christians do. What we call the "Holy Land," they call "the Land of Israel," the former designation being reserved for peculiarly venerated localities.

Even the "Land of Israel" is not always the same as "Holy Land" with us; for Acre is not included, though Caiffa, at the other extremity of the bay, is "holy,"—the former, because the heathen were never driven out of it, the latter, because of being contiguous to Carmel.

The number of Jews in Jerusalem increases annually, more, however, from immigration, than from excess of births over deaths; indeed, the reverse of the latter is the fact, arising from the desire of old people to come and die at Jerusalem.

We should not omit to make mention of the "Jewish Dispensary," (not to be confounded with the larger English hospital for the Jews,) an institution scarcely known but among the Jews of Jerusalem, and mostly, if not entirely, supported by the liberality of Sir Moses Montefiore, Bart., who has so indefatigably laboured in purse and person to ameliorate the condition of his brethren, not only in Jerusalem, but throughout the East.

Of the Sephardim there are nearly 6,000 souls, and of the Ashkenazim nearly 5,000. The Jews have a superstitious objection to make a census; even Sir Moses Montefiore could not obtain one when here; it is founded on 2 Samuel xxiv.

Since these lines were penned, famine, arising from a bad harvest, has been added to the ordinary sufferings of the Jews, and large subscriptions have, as the reader may have noticed, been raised among their wealthier brethren on their behalf.

CHAPTER III.

Interior of the City, Streets, &c.

STREET OF DAVID—DR. ROBINSON'S TYROPEON—BAZAARS—BAB-ES-SALSALA—VIEW FROM WITHIN—STREET OF THE VALLEY—THE BATH "HAMMAM SHEFA"—ARCHWAYS AND FOUNTAIN—THE TEKEEYEH—STREET OF THE PATRIARCH—HOTELS AND CONVENTS OF THE LATINS AND GREEKS—WEST PORCH OF THE CHURCH OF THE HOLY SEPULCHRE—CHURCH OF SEPULCHRE—HOSPITAL OF ST. JOHN—VIA DOLOROSA—CHURCH OF ST. ANNE—POOL OF BETHESDA (SO CALLED)—INTERIOR OF THE HARAM.

The principal street in Jerusalem, for bustle and traffic, is certainly that leading down directly from the Jaffa Gate to the enclosure of the Haram, and which Dr. Robinson supposes to occupy the site of the Tyropeon, or Valley of Cheesemongers, of Josephus, which, according to his account, divided Zion (the Upper City) from Acra (the Lower), and was so deep, that the streets broke off abruptly on either hand. As no valley within the walls at the present day at all answers to this description, we are left to conjecture the site of the original, partly from reasoning and partly from local indications, and in these respects there is certainly much to countenance the views of Dr. Robinson. The street is very narrow, and descends abruptly from the square in front of the citadel. The pavement is execrably rugged; it is bordered by small shops, and thronged by such a crowd of men and women,

ARCHED ST AND FOUNTAIN.

asses and camels, that it is difficult to force one's way, and a total blockade not unfrequently occurs. On descending this street, it is only necessary to take any turning point to the righ*, to see that the brow of Mount Zion rises everywhere steeply above it, a peculiarity entirely omitted in Mr. Williams's *corrected* map of the city. This is not the case, however, on the opposite side, whence the streets that turn off are nearly or quite level. This discrepancy would at once lead us to reject its identity with the Tyropeon of Josephus, were there any other valley offering conditions more closely corresponding with it; but as this is not the case, we are certainly at liberty to infer, that the same accumulation of rubbish which has so greatly disguised the surface of the city, has here also filled up what was formerly a deep and rugged hollow. At all events, if we reject this supposition, we have absolutely no alternative but to extend the limits of Zion over the whole of the high ground occupied by the Church of the Holy Sepulchre, as far as to where it breaks off into the broad and shallow valley traversing the city from the Damascus Gate to Siloam, and which Mr. Williams supposes to be the true Tyropeon, but which at the present day answers as little to the description of Josephus as the other, while it cannot so well be reconciled with the general requirements of the topography.

This street, until its intersection with the bazaars, is called "the Street of David." These bazaars, though highly spoken of in former times, are very inferior to those of Constantinople or Cairo, and present nothing of special interest. On the left-hand side in descending is an old vaulted building, supported on pieces of ancient masonry, now used as a corn-market. After passing the bazaar by a slight bend, the same avenue, now called "the Street of the Temple," is continued to the entrance of the Haram enclosure, at the Bab-es-Salsala, being carried over a causeway, which, according to Mr. Williams's most improbable supposition, was the bridge communicating with Zion, mentioned by Josephus in his account of the siege.

Here let the traveller beware, lest, inadvertently, he finds himself on the very point of entering the forbidden precincts, and is only made aware of his error by the sticks of the sable guardians of the sanctuary,—a fate which has more than once, ere now, befallen the careless or adventurous pilgrim. Just within this gate is a sarcophagus, converted into a cistern, of which I owe a sketch to the kindness of Miss Barclay.

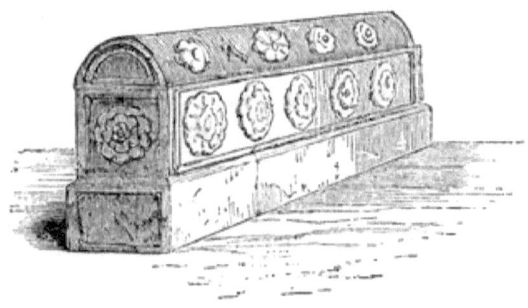

The nearest approach that can be made to the enclosure of the great Mosque is along a street running almost parallel with it, and which, as being the lowest in the city, is called "the Street of the Valley," following the course of the depression or valley traversing the city from the Damascus Gate towards Siloam, and which Mr. Williams believes to be the true Tyropeon of Josephus. In passing along this street, the first turning on the right is the vaulted bazaar, now forsaken and ruinous, which affords access to the Haram by the Bab-el-Katánîn, or Gate of the Cotton Merchants, and of which a bright glimpse is obtained at the end of the gloomy passage. In this ruined bazaar is a bath, called the *Hammam Shefa;* and the idea that the deep well which supplies it might possibly communicate with some of those mysterious reservoirs beneath the Temple, the existence of which has always been fully believed in, induced Mr. Wolcott, one of the American missionaries formerly established here, to undertake the perilous adventure of its exploration. Dr. Robinson, when at Jerusalem, also endeavoured to explore this mysterious well, but was compelled, through various obstacles, to renounce his intention; and it was reserved for another adventurous American (Dr. Barclay) to complete our knowledge of its real nature. "After being several times foiled in my efforts to explore Ain Hammam-es-Shefa (the Bath of Healing), I at last succeeded, a few days ago,—though not without great peril,—in making a thorough examination of its secret recesses. The result, however, is scarcely worth reporting. The theory which ascribes its supply of water to reservoirs under the Haram, is entirely disproved by the exploration. Equally incorrect is the assumption, that it is derived from Gihon fount, or any other extraneous source; and equally fallacious is the idea, that the intermitting flow of the Virgin's fount is owing to an accumulation of water in the reservoir of this fountain, discharged occasionally by a sort of natural syphon. It was found to be a mere *well*, in the ordinary acceptation of that term, without any exit whatever; and the only object of the passage, (supposed to be connected with an unfailing source in the Haram yard) one hundred and four feet of which I succeeded in traversing, and which is eighty-four and a half feet below ground, is to increase guttation, in the direction of the most friable and porous vein of rock, through the internal area from which the water exudes."

Passing the street leading up to Bab-el-Hadid, and also a small ruined fountain, proceeding onward, we shortly reach the point of intersection, another avenue leading across that of "the Valley," up to the enclosure; and here is presented to us, perhaps, the most striking combination of street scenery in Jerusalem. A small fountain of Saracenic architecture, elaborately ornamented, stands at the corner of the street, formerly supplied, as Mr. Williams tells us, by the aqueduct coming from Solomon's Pools at Etham, but affording no longer refreshment to the thirsty passenger, being ruinous and dry, and picturesquely overgrown with the bright and trailing caper-plant. The gate at the end of the street, leading up from it to the Mosque, is called Bab-en-Nazir, or the "Gate of the Inspector." According to the same authority, it formerly bore the name of St. Michael the Archangel, " because, according to the hesitating tradition preserved by an Arabic author, to this gate Gabriel may have bound the celestial beast, Borak, on the night of Mahommed's memorable journey."

In passing this fountain, I was attracted by the babble of childish voices, and, peeping through the grated window of a building just opposite, saw a congregation of children squatted on the ground around a venerable bearded pedagogue, and repeating their lessons. Pursuing the vaulted street, we pass the traditionary house of Saint Veronica, and also that of Dives,— the only objects of any sort of interest till we reach the Damascus Gate.

In the steep and narrow street leading up from this fountain towards the Holy Sepulchre, is the charitable foundation called the *Tekeeyeh*, popularly called the Hospice of St. Helena. The façade of this building is a handsome specimen of Saracenic architecture, but it has fallen greatly to decay in almost every respect: the magnificent edifice is crumbling in heaps, and the vaulted chambers are mostly tenanted by horses of the irregular cavalry service. Food, however, is still distributed there daily to the poor, and strangers go to see the huge caldrons of the kitchen. The food consists only of a kind of gruel, made of flour, water, and oil, without salt; but enough is prepared to supply twice a-day the servants of the Haram, the Tartar and the Indian houses for Moslem pilgrims, besides any poor who may ask for it. The Effendi, who has the administration of its revenues, is said to reap a rich harvest for his trouble.

About four years ago, H. M. the Sultan appointed a French renegade doctor to dispense medicines at the *Tekeeyeh* for the poor, at the expense of the establishment. A public proclamation was made to that effect throughout the city; but the doctor left in a short time, and no more of the matter has been heard of since.

In Mejir-ed-Din, the street is spoken of as Market-street (Akbat-es-Suk), now known as Lady's-street (Akbat-es-Sit), so called from a house built by Dame Tonshok, in 794 (A.D. $139\frac{1}{2}$), who is probably, as Williams suggests, the actual lady benefactress—not Helena; and this supposition is borne out by the Saracenic character of the architecture.

On descending the Street of David, the first turning out of it on the left is that leading to the Holy Sepulchre, and called "the Street of the Patriarch." This avenue displays more appearance of improvement than any other in the city; and contains the offices of the steam-boats touching at Jaffa, one or two Frank stores and shops, and the two hotels already alluded to. That of "The Mediterranean" is a handsome building, and is considered rather more stylish and expensive than the other, which is called the "Hotel de Melita," the proprietor being a Maltese. This building occupies the angle of Patriarch-street, and the steep lane in which is situated the Greek Convent; and though it makes no external show, is airy and comfortable within, the rooms being vaulted and the windows latticed, in the Arabian style; this having been formerly, in fact, the residence of a Turkish Effendi. The upper rooms stand on a terrace, which commands an extensive view over the city. Here I took up my abode during my last visit, and had every reason to be well satisfied with the fare and attentions of mine host.

Indeed, a good inn, in a place like Jerusalem, is no small godsend. It is a real luxury to come home from a ramble over the dusty, glaring hills, or through the foul, fetid lanes and alleys, to the cool, clean terrace, and neatly furnished, comfortable chambers of honest Antonio Zamit. When the heat of the day had subsided, and the declining sun threw a rich rosy light over the city and the Mount of Olives, I always ascended to the level housetop, to enjoy the fresh breeze of the evening, and the melancholy beauty of the outspread view. It was the season of Ramadan, which, as the reader doubtless knows, is the great fast of the Moslems, during which they are prohibited not only from taking food, but, what is perhaps a greater privation, even from smoking, between the rising and setting of the sun. It may be imagined, therefore, with what eagerness they watch the decline of the orb, and listen for the loud booming of the signal-gun from the citadel, which, thrilling through every recess in the city, proclaims the hour of enjoyment. From our airy perch we could then watch them come forth one by one upon the housetop, and resume the beloved pipe, while the servants were preparing their evening meal. The minarets of the city were then illuminated by lamps, the voice of rejoicing ascended on all sides, and feasting and revelry were protracted until a very late hour. But woe to the unlucky traveller who, at this season, after a weary day's work, retires to his couch, in the hope of repairing its fatigues,—especially if his quarters happen, as is here the case, to be immediately above one of the most frequented coffee-houses in the city, where a company of choice spirits are engaged in keeping it up for hours, " braying forth their cozier's catches (as Malvolio says), without any mitigation or remorse of voice." And when these roysterers, at length worn out, begin to drop into silence, and the weary eyes of the traveller to close, then the dogs of the quarter rouse him anew into feverish wakefulness. They are a vile and vagrant race of curs, the very same described by the Psalmist, who " grin" and " go about the city," subsisting on offal and garbage, and reposing by night amidst the endless piles of dirt and rubbish with which Jerusalem abounds. One of these brutes, perhaps half asleep in some corner, is startled by a passing footstep, and instantly breaks forth into a loud hard bark, which speedily arouses his nearest neighbours, these, taking up the chorus, communicate it to the whole slumbering canine population, who, without knowing why or wherefore, rush forth from their obscene

WEST DOOR — CH. OF HOLY SEPULCHRE.

hiding-places, and join battle, till half the city is aroused, and "night made hideous" by the terrific howlings of these belligerent factions. To descend, however, from the top of Antonio's house, we may observe that, just opposite to it, protruding from the wall, by the side of a vaulted archway, which bestrides Patriarch-street, is part of an ancient doorway, now blocked up, being the original western entrance to the Church of the Holy Sepulchre. Half of this is also imbedded in the masonry of the archway which crosses the street. Professor Willis informs us that this door formerly opened directly into the triforium of the church, being on a much higher level than its basement. It is mentioned, he says, by Quaresmius and Edrisi, as being open in their day; and it was walled up by the Turks, together with all other entrances except the present one, in order to facilitate the taking toll of the pilgrims. In architectural style, it resembles the other ancient portions of the church. Through the dark archway is seen part of the Street of the Holy Sepulchre, which, under the name of the Via Dolorosa, descends from the Latin Convent toward St. Stephen's Gate.

We are here in the immediate vicinity of the Greek and Latin Convents, the former adjoining the Holy Sepulchre, and the latter a little above, at the north-west angle of the city, and on the highest ground within its walls. Were we to judge of the moral condition of Jerusalem from the number of its convents and hospitals, we might esteem it to be the most pious and charitable city in the world, where self-renunciation and active benevolence were the only principles that actuated its citizens. In looking at the map, it is surprising how large a space is covered by these monastic buildings.

The establishment of the Latin monks in Palestine is as old as the monastic system itself. Their original seat, Mr. Williams informs us, was the Convent of St. Maria de Latina, established by the merchants of Amalphi, afterwards enlarged into the Hospital of St. John. Being expelled thence by Saladin, they next settled down, when the city was recovered by the Franks, at the Cænaculum, on Mount Zion. A second time driven out, they finally took possession of their present habitation, formerly the seat of the Georgians. Until within a few years, this was not only a shelter for the pilgrims, but the hotel of almost all travellers coming to the Holy City.

The Greek Convent is more exclusive than that of the Latins, as the number of the monks, about one hundred, is considerably greater than that of their rivals.

The principal convent is close to the Malta Hotel, and communicates with the Church of the Sepulchre by an archway carried across Patriarch-street. They have, besides, the Convent of Gethsemane, opposite the south front of the Church of the Holy Sepulchre, and formerly part of the Hospital of St. John; and the Church and Convent of the Forerunner, besides churches for native Christians.

This convent, like the Latin, has its printing-press, which commenced operations at the close of 1852; but hitherto it has been devoted to nothing but church books for common use. It has also its eleemosynary donations to the poor; loaves of bread, from the convent oven, being distributed to the poor at their own houses, every Wednesday and Saturday.

With regard to the Francisan convents in Palestine, besides that of Jerusalem, there are those of Jaffa, Ramlah, Ain Karim (called St. John's), Bethlehem, Acre, and Nazareth. In each of these pilgrims are entertained gratuitously, if they wish it, for three days.

The peculiar central station of the barefooted Carmelites, on Mount Carmel, is independent and distinct from the rest: these allow seven days.

But in Jerusalem a month is allowed, a period of time considered necessary for the Holy City and its adjacent sanctuaries, such as Bethlehem, Ain Karim, and Bethany.

The Convent of Jerusalem is called "St. Salvatore," and the

community is called that of "Terra Santa," administered by a "Procuratore," who is always a Spaniard, and a "Padre Reverendissimo," who is generally Italian: the latter is chosen by the General of the order in Rome, and changed every three years. Formerly there was a French Vicar, but this office has ceased since there have been no French monks in Palestine, and no receipt of French money.

All Latin convents in the East are placed under protection of the French Consulates, according to the well-known title assumed by the French interest in Turkey,—that of "Protector of Christianity." Of course, this protection is only available for those who choose to accept it.

The Terra Santa Convent, in Jerusalem, is said to possess enormous wealth in sacerdotal utensils and vestments, exceeding that of the Greeks and Armenians.

In connexion with the Latin Patriarchates are the following institutions:—

1. The *Patriarch's Hospital* was opened in 1851, chiefly by the efforts and means of the public-spirited Chancellor of the French Consulate, M. Lequeux, and the talented assistance of A. Mendelsohn, M.D.

This is a general hospital for relief of all persons without distinction. Each department, male or female, has a ward apart for non-Roman Catholics, who might not wish to participate in religious offices with that communion. Since the establishment has been placed directly under the Latin Patriarchate, it is become much deteriorated in efficiency. Its earliest physician having left the country, the medical officer at present is not of the class that was at first intended.

2. *St. Vincent de Paul.*—A committee has been recently formed among the Roman Catholic Europeans of Jerusalem, in connexion with the celebrated Society of that name in Paris. Its object is to administer relief to the sick, to prisoners, and to cases of distress generally: it is supported by voluntary contributions.

3. *Sisters of Charity.*—A branch of the Lazarist Society, under that name, commenced operations in 1850. The Sisters are now ten in number, and their attentions are not limited to the hospital of the Patriarchate. They conduct a girls' school in Jerusalem, which is well attended.

4. *Seminary* and *Day-School.*—The former of these, attached to the Patriarchate, contains fourteen students, wearing a scholastic dress of purple. Most of them have hitherto been brought from the Jesuit or Lazarist establishments of Lebanon, already prepared by some education for this seminary.

5. *Printing-press.*—Exceedingly well carried on, in Latin, Italian, and Arabic: mostly employed on works of religious character, and annual almanacs.

6. *General Charity.*—The Convent of Terra Santa dispenses loaves of bread to the poor every Tuesday and Saturday, at their own houses. A number of wells within its walls are reserved for the poor in times of unusual drought, and all the families of the community have houses provided *gratis.*

Connected with the Latin Patriarchate is the celebrated *Propaganda Society* of Rome, the agents of which are men of learning and talent.

A little way down Patriarch-street, in the opposite direction, is Palmer-street, a narrow winding lane or passage, which leads down into the square court in front of the Church of the Holy Sepulchre, and from thence gives access to the bazaars. This, as commanding the chief avenue to this venerated spot, is the chosen stand from whence the vendors of that holy ware—the fabrication of which employs a large number of the Christian inhabitants of the city and neighbourhood—pounce upon the passing pilgrim; and rarely does the traveller so pass without being hailed by one of these "traffickers in holy things," anxious to tempt him with rosaries of beads, whether of olive-wood from the sacred Mount, of sandal-wood, or black, and red, and white pearl,—with crosses of every size, from small ones of plain olive, to others a foot long, elaborately and often very cleverly carved in pearl,—with cups and bowls made of the bitumen of the Dead Sea,—and other similar valuables, all of them duly consecrated at the sacred tomb; a trade as thriving in Jerusalem as the making of silver shrines to Diana was of old in Ephesus, and, it is to be feared, too frequently associated with a devotion of very similar character.

Descending rather steeply from these receptacles of pious ware, we enter the square paved court in front of the Church of the Holy Sepulchre. We shall not here open the inquiry as to the genuineness of the site. In the "Walks about Jerusalem" it is observed, that upon merely topographical grounds we could see no objection to it." But while of course admitting, in the uncertainty which hangs over all questions of the kind, the bare *possibility* that the spot thus consecrated might be without the second wall, yet the more the question is considered, and the ground reexamined, the more *improbable* does it seem that such can ever have been the case. And, forcible as may at first appear the argument drawn from tradition, it is greatly weakened when we take into account the palpable errors in fixing certain other sacred localities, and their transference from one spot to another, to say nothing of the pious frauds and barefaced impositions, of which Jerusalem in general, and this church in particular, can show so plentiful a stock.

Leaving, then, this interminable question for others to dispose of, according to the bias of their minds, we propose here merely to give a few brief notices of the building in its past and present condition. In so doing, we shall take for granted that it stands upon the site originally selected, and repudiate altogether Mr. Ferguson's theory of the transference of the locality from the Mosque of Omar to this spot.

Eusebius affirms that there was no difficulty in finding the sacred tomb, when Constantine desired to build a church over it, because "impious men and the whole race of demons" had covered it up with earth and had desecrated it by the erection of a temple to Venus. The earth being removed, the tomb was discovered, and is described as "a cave that had evidently been hewn out of the rock,"—"a rock standing out erect and alone on a level land, and having only one cavern in it." The cave was then cut externally into shape, adorned with columns, and surmounted with a cross. A round church was erected over it, adjacent to which was also a Basilica, the porch of which opened upon the market-place of the city. When the Persians sacked Jerusalem, they reduced these buildings to a state of ruin, but they were not long after restored by Modestus. Of the appearance of the tomb at that time, we have numerous accounts by the early pilgrims. Arculf describes it as being "a circular vault cut all out of one and the same rock, wherein *nine* men could stand up and pray, with a clear foot and a half over their heads. The entrance was on the east. The exterior was encrusted with marble, and had a large golden cross on the top. In the northern part of the vault was the tomb, cut out of the same rock as the vault itself, but higher up than the floor. The *inside* had no decoration, but showed the marks of the chisel, and the colour was piebald, or of a mingled red and white.

And thus it remained until Jerusalem was ravaged by the fanatic caliph, Hakem, who ordered the churches to be a second time dismantled. It is a question whether the sepulchre itself was destroyed on this occasion. That laborious efforts were made to get rid of it is upon record, but it is doubtful whether they proved successful. The advocates for the genuineness of the site are divided on this point; Schultz believing that the tomb was destroyed, Williams that it still remained, though in a mutilated condition. The caliph, however, within a few months, ordered the churches to be rebuilt, which was immediately effected; so that in any case the sepulchre, even if broken down, was of course restored upon its original site.

The pilgrims, Sœwulf and others, now speak of the *interior*, formerly left bare, as *being covered with rich marble*, from which it is evident that the building had been so broken and defaced, that it had been found necessary to coat it over. Further damage was inflicted by the Kharismian hordes, when they sacked Jerusalem in 1244. The monument was falling into ruin when repaired by Father Bonifacius in 1555, at the instance of the Emperor Charles V. The masonry was taken down, when *the tomb* came to light; not, that is to say, the circular vault described by Arculf, for that had been probably broken away, but merely that portion in which the body was deposited. It is not very clear how much was done to it by Bonifacius. But not only the sepulchre, but the group of buildings enclosing and surrounding it, have undergone numerous transformations. Constantine erected a round church over the sepulchre, and finding the rise of the rocky ground to the westward (which is still distinctly to be traced) inconvenient for building upon, he erected to the eastward a splendid Basilica, with a fine porch. These edifices were totally destroyed by the Persians under Chosroes.

In the restoration by Modestus, already alluded to, the symmetrical arrangement of the original buildings was not observed; but the group included churches of the Resurrection, of the Sepulchre, the Calvary, and St. Constantine; and many new sites of different incidents of the Saviour's sufferings were now, for the first time, added by the credulous spirit of the age. The Chapel of Helena is supposed by Professor Willis to belong to this period. In the restoration that took place after the destruction by Hakim, still further modifications occurred. But the present complicated and intricate jumble of buildings owed its form to the Crusaders. When they took possession of Jerusalem, they found that certain of the holy places, such as the Golgotha, and the place of the Invention of the Cross, were merely small oratories outside the principal church. Not satisfied with this state of things, they went to work, and ingeniously included the whole beneath one roof; and these arrangements have remained undisturbed, except by the fire of 1808, which having destroyed the interior of the Round Church, it was recased again two years afterwards.

The southern front of the church, with the massive campanile, has formed the subject of such numerous illustrations that we shall not reproduce it here. It is a strikingly picturesque and venerable façade, in what Professor Willis calls " Pointed Romanesque," the doors and windows being loaded with rich ornament, in a mixed and peculiar style. The campanile has a somewhat ponderous appearance, from the loss of the two upper stories, which must formerly have rendered it a very handsome tower. It stands over the Chapel of St. John. Connected with it, and forming the western side of the court, is a range of chapels, the apses of which externally appear as buttresses. Attached to the south-western angle, is to be seen one of a range of columns, which, now broken off, once ran across the court, forming a portico to the adjacent buildings.

On entering the western door, the first object after the Turk, who is stationed on the left to take toll, is the *Stone of Unction;* to the right of which is the *Chapel of Adam, or Godfrey,* with the tombs of Godfrey de Bouillon and his successor Baldwin I. A flight of steps a little to the right ascends to the *Chapel of Calvary,* which is not much more than one hundred feet from the Sepulchre itself. Here is to be seen the rock with the holes for the three crosses. This rock stood formerly in the open air, and the crosses were erected upon it.

Descending again past the Stone of Unction, we bear to the left, and enter the Great Rotunda, under the centre of which stands the Sepulchre. It should be borne in mind, that the floor is here much below the level of Patriarch-street, so that, as before remarked, the western door in that street, now blocked up, formerly opened into the *triforium,* or second story of the Rotunda. This was in existence when the Crusaders took Jerusalem, and was a beautiful specimen of Byzantine architecture, with mosaics on a gilt ground; but its appearance has been lamentably altered by the great fire of 1808, which completely destroyed the roof and surface, and the new casing is excessively ponderous and ugly.

At the west end of the Rotunda, forming, before the fire, part of the aisle, is the altar of the Syrians, through which is a passage into a very singular excavation in the rock; certainly very much resembling one of the tombs in the neighbourhood of the city. It is observed with reason, by Professor Willis, that this serves to accredit the idea, that the sloping rock of the hillside in which this sepulchre is carved may have extended further eastward, so as to have also included the Holy Sepulchre.

Of the former state of the Sepulchre we have already spoken. At present.it resembles but little that described by Eusebius and seen by Arculf. No portion of the original rock is visible; but the whole structure appears to be artificially built up.

Opening from the Rotunda, and in a line with it, is the Greek Church, forming the choir of the original building, formerly belonging to the Latins, and terminated by a semicircular apse. The Greeks, who obtained possession of it after its recovery from the Saracens, have disguised its primitive appearance by an enormous screen splendidly adorned and gilt after their manner; as is this entire portion of the building, over which rises the lantern cupola, so conspicuous on the exterior.

The sombre Church of the Latins, or, as it is called, Chapel of the Virgin Mary of the Apparition, which branches off from the north-east corner of the Rotunda, will not sustain a comparison with the gorgeous glitter of that of the Greeks. But it may vie with, if it does not surpass it, in spurious holy places; for here, in the vestibule are to be seen the place where our Lord appeared in the likeness of a gardener to Mary Magdalene; also, where the latter stood; while within the little church itself is the spot where Jesus appeared to his mother after the Resurrection, the place of the Recognition of the Cross, with part of the pillar to

8

which the Redeemer was bound. Pretty well for a nook about sixty feet long by twenty! These legendary localities, it is but fair to explain, were gradually accumulated around that of the Sepulchre, as mediæval darkness became more dense, and the credulity of the pilgrims more craving, and the fraud of the priests more barefaced.

From the vestibule of the Latin Church, and going along the aisle of the choir, to the Greek church towards the apse, we have a range of fine pillars and capitals, as old probably as any part of the existing edifice; and here is a similar basket-shaped capital to that cited by Mr. Ferguson, from the Mosque of Omar, as being peculiarly Saracenic. At the north-east corner of the inner aisle is the Chapel of the Virgin. Following the curve of the apse, we have first a niche called the Chapel of Longinus the Centurion. A little further, and in the centre of the curve, the Chapel of the Parting of our Lord's Garments; and the symmetry of these chapels is kept up by a third on the other side, which is called the Chapel of the Mocking.

Between these two last chapels a dark staircase of forty-nine steps leads down into what is at the present day the most strikingly picturesque and impressive portion of this curious agglomeration of buildings. This is the Chapel of Helena, to which allusion has already been made. It is nearly square, and above the centre is a cupola with four small windows which dimly light up the sombre edifice. The pillars and capitals are ponderously picturesque, in a rude Byzantine style, different from any other part of the buildings. The pavement is broken and rugged, and the whole place damp and gloomy, being built on the site of a dry cistern. Silver lamps are suspended here and there from the roof, and festoons of ostrich eggs are slung from pillar to pillar.

Finally, by a steep flight of thirteen steps at its south-east corner, we descend into the dark vault called the "Chapel of the Invention of the Cross." Here, in the very heart of the rock, the moisture exuding from which was converted by the fancy of

CHAPEL OF HELENA & CAVE OF THE CROSS

superstitious pilgrims into tears wept for sorrow at our Lord's sufferings, is an altar over which several lamps are suspended, serving but faintly to irradiate the cavernous gloom. Here were dug up the three Crosses, and all the accessories of the Crucifixion, such as the crown of thorns, the nails, and the inscription over the cross, under the inspection of the pious Helena, who, as tradition tells us, sat in a marble chair, preserved in the chapel above, to superintend the operation.

The Church of the Sepulchre is opened at certain hours for the performance of divine service, though admission may be gained at other times by application at the neighbouring convent. I preferred to visit it, in company with my French fellow-traveller, at the hour of vespers. I cannot describe the mingled emotions by which I was agitated during our perambulation of this most singular edifice. Its venerable antiquity and gorgeous gloom— its dim recesses and mysterous corridors—its silver lamps and pictures of saints—the clouds of incense—the organ echoing through the lofty vault—the solemn chant of the monks—could not but produce a solemn and affecting influence, and call to mind the long series of pilgrims, monks, and warriors, who during so many centuries had worshipped around the Sacred Tomb. On the other hand, in looking at the dark unintellectual faces of the monks, redolent of ignorance and fanaticism—*des "vrais brigands,"* as my French friend, with all his piety, correctly denominated them; the evidently formal and ritual character of their worship; everything connected with the place seem to bear the dark stamp of a superstition little, if at all, better than that of the old Pagans. Upon some of those monkish figures one could not look without an actual shudder. One miserable creature in particular riveted our attention, and is ineffaceably stamped upon the memory, as bringing before the eye the very figure of an anchoret of the middle ages. He was an Abyssinian monk, and exactly resembled a reanimated mummy; his body was shrunk to the mere bone, and the dark brown skin seemed drawn over it like parchment; his vacant eye was deeply sunk, his face totally devoid of any expression but that of the most abject superstition. His whole dress consisted of a loose robe of blue serge, which hung about his emaciated body like a shroud. In his hand was a psalter which he continued to mutter with lifeless mechanical devotion. His whole appearance so betokened the very extreme of indigence, if not of actual starvation, that neither of us could refrain from bestowing on him a small alms.

In perambulating this church, and seeing its every hole and corner occupied by figures such as these—by different sets of warring monks, regarding one another with deadly hatred, exhausting every artifice of petty intrigue to supplant each other in the possession of these gainful shrines, and often coming to open blows in the very holiest places, there is something so melancholy and degrading in the spectacle, that one almost wishes that the place was levelled to the ground, and its dust dispersed to the winds; that Christianity might no longer be thus dishonoured and degraded on the very spot where it first came into existence.

In the narrow street leading from the Church of the Sepulchre towards the bazaars, stands a curious and very picturesque gateway, the external façade displaying a flattened pointed arch, somewhat similar to that at the Tomb of the Virgin, while the archway beyond is round-headed, having formerly a round arched portal surmounted by rich historical and emblematical carving. Among the varied and curious ornaments above may be seen the Lamb, emblem of the noble order of St. John of Jerusalem, of whose palace this was the entry. Fallen are the mighty indeed, and degraded their dwelling-place; for, of all spots in the city, this is at present the most filthy and disgusting, owing to a neighbouring tannery and certain cesspools, which create together a stench sufficient, one would think, to breed a pestilence in the neighbourhood, and which render a prolonged examination of these interesting relics almost impossible.

Behind the gateway are seen, in the sketch, some remains of the building. The interior is now converted to the basest uses, and not to be explored without considerable offence to the nostrils, and the fear of catching some infectious disorder from contact with the wretches who vegetate in filth and misery, amid the ruined cloisters of these gallant and noble knights. From the open area a picturesque staircase ascends to a court surrounded by a cloister, from which open sundry rooms, into which it is hardly possible to penetrate for various disgusting obstructions. One large building with painted windows, either the hall or chapel, is now nearly filled up with dung.

This building stood in immediate proximity to a splendid group of religious foundations, thus described by Sæwulf in 1102:—" Without the gate of the Holy Sepulchre, to the south, is the Church of St. Mary, called the Latin, because the monks there perform divine service in the Latin tongue. And the Assyrians say that the blessed mother of our Lord, at the crucifixion of her Son, stood on the spot now occupied by the altar of this church. Adjoining to this church is another Church of St. Mary, called the Little, occupied by nuns, who serve devoutly the Virgin and her Son, near which is the Hospital, where is a celebrated monastery founded in honour of St. John the Baptist."

The building is thus described by Mandeville, in 1322:— " Before the Church of St. Sepulchre, 200 paces to the south, is the great Hospital of St. John, of which the Hospitallers had their foundation. And within the palace of the sick men of that hospital are 124 pillars of stone, and in the walls of the house, besides the number aforesaid, there are fifty-four pillars that support the house. From that hospital, going towards the east, is a very fair church, which is called Our Lady the Great, and after it there is another church, very near, called Our Lady the Latin; and there stood Mary Cleophas and Mary Magdalene, and tore their hair when our Lord was executed on the cross."

The important part played by this noble body of knights, not onl in Palestine, but afterwards at Rhodes and Malta, gives peculiar interest to these mouldering memorials of their former power and splendour, in the city where the order originated, and whence it derived its name, and may justify the insertion of a few historical details, extracted from the writer's "Overland Route," in which the fortunes of the order are traced from their origin to their ruin.

"It was in the eleventh century, that a few merchants from Amalphi, now an obscure but romantic town in the vicinity of Naples, but at that time famous for the enterprise of its citizens (by one of whom the mariners' compass was discovered), obtained permission of the Moslem caliphs to establish, under the shadow of the Church of the Holy Sepulchre, a place of refuge for pilgrims of both sexes visiting Jerusalem. Two hospitals, one for male pilgrims, dedicated to St. John Elymon, the other to the Holy Magdalene, formed the cradle of the celebrated order of St. John at Jerusalem. Scarcely had it existed seventeen years, when a terrible irruption of the Turcomans swept Jerusalem with the besom of destruction; the Moslem troops were massacred, and the tributary Christian population, hitherto permitted to exist uneasily within the walls of the Holy City, were exposed to the most cruel outrages. Peter the Hermit, beholding the sufferings endured by his brethren, overran Europe, inflaming its chivalry to roll back the advancing tide of Mahomedan conquest; the first crusade was undertaken, and ere long Godfrey of Bouillon stood victorious upon the ramparts of the Holy City.

"On visiting the Hospital of St. John, soon after his conquest, he was received by the pious Gerard, who, having witnessed the charity of its inmates, had devoted himself and his fortune to their service; and by his benevolent care of the pilgrims, without distinction of sect, and the extension of his bounty even to the infidels themselves, was regarded as a common father by all the poor of the city. His example inspired many of the young nobles with a kindred spirit, who, renouncing the idea of returning to their homes, enrolled themselves among the Hospitallers. Godfrey endowed them with lands, and most of the other crusading princes following his example, the order was soon enriched with considerable possessions both in Europe and in Palestine. Hitherto the Hospitallers had confined themselves to an administration merely secular; they now, at the persuasion of Gerard, added to it a religious profession, took the three vows of poverty, chastity, and obedience, and assumed a regular habit, consisting of a plain black robe, upon which, at the side next the heart, was attached an eight-pointed cross of white linen. The Pope, approving of this new order, exempted the Hospitallers from the payment of tithes, and bestowed on them the exclusive right of electing their own superior, without the interference of either secular or ecclesiastical powers. The wealth and influence of the institution now increased apace, and they founded hospitals or commanderies in the principal maritime provinces of Europe, where pilgrims to Jerusalem were succoured and sent forward on their journey.

"Such was the origin of this famous order; first merely a civil, and next a religious institution for the succour of pilgrims repairing to Palestine. But the establishment of the Latin kingdom of Jerusalem brought on a further change in its constitution. A mere handful of Christian knights, surrounded by hosts of Moslem enemies, could not afford to spare the valiant knights at present bound by a purely religious vow; and Raymond Depuy, the successor of Gerard, proposed that those who had laid down their arms should assume them again for the defence of their newly-founded and precarious state. The body of Hospitallers was now divided into three classes;—the first, of noble birth and approved valour, were destined to military service; the second consisted of priests and almoners; while a third and inferior class, who had no pretensions to nobility of origin, assumed the functions of ' Frères Servans,' or assistants; and as the number of the order was rapidly swelled by an influx of youthful knighthood from all parts of Europe, it was further divided into seven languages,—those, namely, of Provence, Auvergne, France, Italy, Aragon, Germany, and England; a division which, with the addition of Castile and Portugal, subsisted until the extinction of the order, except that after the Reformation the English lodge was merged in the German. The government was a pure aristocracy, the supreme authority residing in a council, of which the Grand Master was the chief.

" This order of the Knights Hospitallers of St. John, together with that of the Templars, which not long after sprung from it, were the principal support to the Latin kingdom of Jerusalem, during the brief period through which it struggled in the midst of peril and uncertainty. Our space will not allow us to dwell upon the many signal proofs of their prowess which were given during their residence in Palestine. They presented a singular union of military valour with religious fervour and austerity of life. 'Scarcely,' says Vertot, 'had they laid down their arms, than they resumed, with the utmost regularity, all the exercise of their first profession. Some devoted themselves to the service of the sick, or were occupied with receiving pilgrims, while others kept their arms in order, or with their own hands mended the harness of their war horses; and during these various employments maintained a religious silence, like hermits or anchorets,—a manner of life hitherto unparalleled, when, without being entirely attached to the cloister, nor engaged in the world, they practised in succession all the virtues of two such opposite conditions.' Such were the Hospitallers during the first period of their institution, which may be regarded as the golden age of their order: but this state of things continued for little more than a century; the spirit of the warrior gradually encroached upon that of the monk; and the desire of riches, the love of pleasure, or the thirst for distinction, began to infect an order founded on a vow of humility and poverty. Their valour,

however, suffered no eclipse; and, after bearing an honourable and prominent part in the vain struggle to maintain the Holy Land against the overwhelming hosts of the Saracens, at the final siege of Acre, in 1291, and whilst in the midst of conflagration and carnage, a dreadful slaughter took place of the Templars, John de Villiers, the Grand Master, and a devoted band, covered the retreat of the handful of their brethren who survived, and, getting on board a carrack belonging to their order, escaped to Limisso, in Cyprus; 'and a touching spectacle it was,' in the words of their historian, Vertot, 'to behold these valiant knights, all covered with wounds, descend from their vessels upon a foreign strand, with countenances suited to their altered fortunes, and overwhelmed with sorrow that they should have outlived the total loss of the Holy Land.'"

The subsequent fortunes of the order hardly need recapitulation. They established themselves at Rhodes, and erected those noble fortifications which the traveller still views with so much admiration. Expelled by an overwhelming body of Turks, and again scattered abroad, they next settled at Malta, which, in their hands, speedily became all but impregnable. Here they long remained the bulwark of Christendom against the Turks, till, weakened by internal decline, they at length ingloriously surrendered to Buonaparte, and the order was finally dissolved.

The Templars—who so long bore with them the brunt of the struggle against the Saracens—were originally so called from their being lodged in the Mosque-el-Aksa, within the precincts of the temple area. In front of the porch of this mosque—it is not generally known—are buried the murderers of St. Thomas à Becket, who died at Jerusalem, upon a pilgrimage undertaken in expiation of their crime.

The upper part of the long street descending from the Latin Convent to St. Stephen's Gate is called the Street of the Holy Sepulchre, the lower, the "Via Dolorosa," or "Dolorous Way," from the tradition that Jesus, after being condemned by Pilate, (probably at the Fort Antonia, or Governor's Palace,) was forced to toil up its steep acclivity, laden with his cross, to the place of crucifixion on Calvary. Although, supposing the modern streets to occupy the line of the ancient ones, there is sufficient verisimilitude about this tradition to render it, at least, striking to the imagination of the pilgrim, yet there is little doubt that the tradition, and the poetical name of the street, originated in the monkish ages, in connexion with the Church of the Sepulchre, and its supposititious rock of Calvary.

But, however this may be, this street is the most gloomily impressive of any within the precincts of this melancholy city. Descending from the angle of Patriarch-street, at the corner, and adjacent to the Church of the Sepulchre, is a tall and elegant minaret and mosque, called El Khanky, formerly the residence of the Latin Patriarch. Of this building a curious tale is related by Mejir-ed-Din, that the Christians were excessively distressed at seeing this minaret arising in such close proximity to the Holy Sepulchre, which it entirely commanded. They offered a large sum to Sheik Ibn Ghanem, to bribe him to desist; but he persisted, and completed the structure. Mahomet then appeared to a man, whom he commanded to salute Ibn Ghanem, and assure him of his intercession at the day of judgment, for the meritorious work of having outtopped the infidels.

Hence we descend gradually to the intersection of the covered bazaar, which traverses the city in a line due north, to the Damascus Gate, and along which, at various points, Mr. Williams and others have fancied they have discovered vestiges of the old second wall of Josephus. One of these imaginary traces occurs at this point of intersection, in part of the vaulted street to which Mr. Williams has given the imposing name of " Porta Judicii," and the antique character of which appeared to me to be grossly exaggerated in his annexed illustration. But in spite of the long list of names with which he fortifies his opinion, I must confess myself unable to discover any reasonable foundation for it, or to regard these remains as having anything distinctive about them.

Hence the narrow street descends more rapidly, sometimes open to the sky, at others diving between a succession of gloomy archways. The pavement is rugged and slippery as a mountain road; the prison-like walls on either side are only pierced here and there by a small doorway or grated window, or a wooden "jalousie," or lattice. In the shade of the archways the passenger stumbles over heaps of stones and rubbish, or is half blinded with clouds of dust, while vapours indescribably fetid escape from holes and corners, and assail his nostrils. We have endeavoured to convey the character of this singularly gloomy street scenery in a study taken on the spot, in which the effect of light and shade is closely copied from nature. As may be supposed, at twilight these archways are involved in utter darkness; and, unless provided with a lantern, it is difficult to grope one's way without treading upon a sleeping dog, or coming into violent collision with some invisible passenger.

After descending and crossing the street of the valley which intersects the city from the Damascus Gate, the Via Dolorosa ascends slightly as far as the Governor's house, passing under a round arch of Roman fragments, bearing the traditional name of the "Ecce Homo" arch, from the evidently baseless tradition that Pilate from thence displayed Jesus to the populace.

On the left hand, near this spot, is the Church of the Flagellation.

The street now slopes gradually downward, passing under a pointed archway, surmounting some evidently ancient stonework, represented in Mr. Williams's work, and unhesitatingly called by him part of the Tower of Antonia. A little beyond is a turning giving access to the Haram enclosure; on approaching which, somewhat incautiously, I was saluted with a shower of stones from some Moslem boys. Still descending a short distance, on the left is the Church of St. Anne, recently restored, and an interesting specimen of the Christian pointed architecture of Jerusalem. Various notices of this building may be gleaned from the early travellers. Among others, Sæwulf, who visited Palestine A.D. 1102, says: " From the Temple of the Lord, you go to the church of St. Anne, the mother of the blessed Mary, towards the north, where she lived with her husband, and she was there delivered of her daughter Mary. Near it is the pool called in Hebrew, Bethesda, having five porticoes, of which the Gospel speaks. A little above is the place where the woman was healed by our Lord, by touching the hem of his garment, while he was surrounded by a crowd in the street." Sir John Mandeville, A.D. 1322, says: ".Without the cloister of the Temple, toward the north, is a very fair church of St. Anne, our Lady's mother; and there our Lady was conceived. And before that church is a great tree, which began to grow the same night. And under that church, on going down by twenty-two steps, lies Joachim, our Lady's father, in a fair tomb of stone; and there beside lay sometime St. Anne, his wife; but St. Helena caused her to be translated to Constantinople. And in that church is a well, in manner of a cistern, which is called *Probatica Piscina*, which hath five entrances. Angels used to come from heaven into that well, and bathe them in it; and the man who first bathed after the moving of the water, was made whole," &c. Here it would seem doubtful whether the worthy knight is not confounding this in his recollection with the neighbouring cistern under the Haram wall, traditionally considered as the Pool of Bethesda. But Mr. Williams informs us, that there was formerly another large tank before this church, described as above by the pilgrims, but now dried up. If it be so, it only serves to show with what facility the names of sacred localities—originally given without reason—are at a subsequent period lost, and transferred elsewhere.

After the Saracen conquest, this establishment was endowed as a college and hospital by Saladin.

Maundrell speaks of the church as being in his day (1697) "large and entire, and so are part of the lodgings; but both are desolate and neglected. In a grotto under the church is shown the place where they say the blessed Virgin was born."

When Mr. Catherwood was at Jerusalem, in 1820, he made the annexed sketch of the buildings, with which he has been so

kind as to favour me. It will be seen that the tower, which is no longer standing, was distinctively Gothic, and that the buildings of the convent were then built up against it. Part of a wall with Gothic buttresses, forming, probably, the external enclosure, forms the foreground of this interesting sketch—one of the most curious memorials of the crusading times in Jerusalem.

At the time when Dr. Robinson visited Jerusalem, he describes this edifice as dilapidated, but it has since been *restored* by the Turks, or rather metamorphosed into a new form, which it would puzzle the archæologist to explain. It is, however, still surrounded with heaps of rubbish and ruinous vaults. The pointed architecture and Byzantine dome would show distinctively its Christian origin, even without the notices collected from the early writers and pilgrims by Robinson, as well as those already cited. From these we learn, that William of Tyre speaks of "the House of Anna on this spot, as a place where three or four old women had consecrated themselves to a monastic life." Jacob de Vitry says, "It was called the Abbey of St. Anne, and was inhabited by an abbess and black nuns, *i. e.* of the Benedictine order." The ruined vaults around most probably formed part of the conventual buildings.

The most extensive ancient pool within the city is undoubtedly that close to St. Stephen's Gate. Its dimensions, according to Robinson, are "360 feet in length, 130 feet in breadth, and 75 feet in depth to the bottom, besides the rubbish which has been accumulating in it for ages." The common tradition calls it the Pool of Bethesda, though certainly without any foundation whatever, beyond the assumed identity of St. Stephen's Gate with the Sheep Gate, near which the aforesaid pool was situated. A glance at the annexed view of it will show that it has long been dry, and used as a receptacle for rubbish, large fig-trees having struck their roots into the soil. On the south side it forms the boundary of the Haram enclosure, the wall of which, surmounted by a minaret, rises above the top of the pool itself. Along the east side passes the roadway from St. Stephen's Gate to the Mosque, the edge of which appears in the foreground. Northward, it is bounded by a few houses and ruins extending along the Via Dolorosa, a path from which is seen descending into the area, between an overgrowth of prickly pear. The western side is remarkable for the two large arches sustaining the picturesque pile of buildings above, which, like the pool itself, are blocked up with accumulated soil. Dr. Robinson was, however, able to measure 100 feet within the northern one, and it appeared to him to stretch much further. Looking at the great length and depth of this excavation, he is inclined to regard it as the defensive trench which divided Fort Antonia and the Temple from the rocky ridge of Bezetha. This trench would have been partly filled up by the ruins of the Fort, after it was stormed and levelled by Titus, and might afterwards have been converted into a pool, unless, indeed, it originally served that purpose also. That it was used for it at some time, is apparent from the traces of cement upon its sides.

CHAPTER IV.

The Mount of Olives and the Valley of Jehoshaphat.

TOWER ON THE MOUNT—CHURCH OF THE ASCENSION—ANCIENT TRADITIONS—PANORAMIC VIEW OF JERUSALEM—GARDEN OF GETHSEMANE ALTERED—TRADITIONS—TOMB OF ABSALOM—POOL OF THE VIRGIN—ISAIAH'S TREE—EN ROGEL—ROCK TOMBS AND ACELDAMA.

On revisiting Jerusalem, the first wish of the pilgrim will ever be to reascend the Mount of Olives, to wander among its sacred groves, and from its breezy top to overlook the city,—realizing anew the solemn and affecting scenes of the New Testament narrative. Bewildered as he is within the city itself,—by the conflicting theories of antiquaries, until there is scarcely a single monument or stone about the origin of which he can venture to be positive,—it is refreshing to go forth without the walls, and recognise, beyond all peradventure, amidst the unchangeable forms of the ancient hills and glens, the very ground rendered sacred by the footsteps of the Redeemer, the groves amidst which he found shelter and retirement, and the pathways he was accustomed to traverse with his disciples in his way to Bethany. And besides the halo of melancholy and of glory which must for ever clothe the summit of this sacred Mount, it is in itself by far the pleasantest—one might almost say, the only

pleasant spot in the environs of the Holy City. Though no longer thickly covered with the tree from which it derives its name, it possesses yet more shade and verdure than any other part of the neighbourhood; and the view of Jerusalem from its sides and summit is incomparably the finest that can anywhere be obtained.

Another advantage it has, which was of no small importance at this period of my visit. The intense heats of summer had now set in, and the close streets and ill-drained houses of the city had become so unhealthy, that many European families retreated without the walls, either occupying such country-houses as were obtainable, or, in default of these, pitching their tents at some chosen retreat in the environs. Now, no place could be better suited for this purpose than the Mount of Olives. At a time when those in the city were panting with close heat, and half-stifled with fetid exhalations, the pure, fresh breezes were coursing freely over the hill-sides, bracing the relaxed nerves and raising the spirits of Europeans, as far as is anywhere possible during the ardours of a Syrian summer.

It was my good fortune at this juncture to fall in with an American family, who had abandoned for awhile their house in the city, and established themselves upon the side of the Mount. Their quarters consisted of an old dilapidated Saracenic tower, and a few tents grouped around it. It stood upon one of those rocky projections with which the Mount is studded. The lower story consisted of a ruinous apartment, and a broken stairway giving access to a vaulted chamber above, with two small windows, which served as the general sitting-room. The walls were rough and half ruinous; but a few divans and articles of furniture, with books, portfolios, and mathematical instruments, gave it a somewhat habitable appearance. But the charm to me was in the unaffected kindness and superior intelligence of its inmates; and as I toiled, under a blazing sun, up the steep pathway, pausing every now and then under the shade of a gnarled olive, I felt that every step brought me nearer to what was really a temporary home in a foreign land.

The situation of this tower is, I think, unequalled for the view it commands, not only of the city, and especially of the great platform of the Temple (which is here seen in the finest relief), but of the principal slope of the Mount of Olives itself, the buildings on its summit, and the gloomy valley of Jehoshaphat unrolled at its base. It was the only spot from which one might realise what there is of grandeur and impressiveness on the site of Jerusalem. Beautiful when the morning sun, rising above the mountains of Arabia, diffused a brilliant light over the opposite eastern walls, and on the domes and towers of the city, it was far more striking when the luminary, about to sink in the opposite direction, cast a rich slanting glow along the level grassy area and marble platform of the Temple enclosure, touching with gold the edge of the beautiful Dome of the Rock, and the light arabesque fountains with which the area is studded; while the eastern walls and the deep valley below are thrown into a deep and solemn shadow, creeping, as the orb sank lower, further and further towards the summit, irradiated with one parting gleam of roseate light, after all below was sunk into obscurity. It was the same hour, as we know, when Jesus was accustomed to steal forth from the city, and commune with his Father among the shady gardens at the foot of the Holy Mount.

The first walk with my American friend was to the old Mosque and ruinous Church of the Ascension, which crown the summit of the hill. Passing across slopes, thinly covered with barley, and shaded by detached clumps of olive and fig-trees, we struck into the path leading directly from St. Stephen's Gate to the top, and soon entered the Mosque, when its keeper, an old Turk, who knew the "Hadgi Americana," received us with great civility. The view from the gallery of the minaret is widely extensive, but less clear and explanatory than might be supposed, on account of some intervening ground. On one side lay the city, looking, from this height, like a huge model in relief, upon its sloping platform; but, as others have remarked, not seen to so much advantage as from various points lower down the hill. The eye wandered in all directions over the rugged hill-country of Judea, and the desolate volcanic mountains hemming in the Dead Sea, a portion of which was visible.

Of all the traditions of Jerusalem and its environs, the one which seems most palpably to contradict the plain letter of the New Testament, is that which places the scene of the Ascension on the summit of Mount Olivet. The statement in St. Luke's Gospel is, that "Jesus led out his disciples as far as to Bethany, and blessed them, and when he blessed them, he was parted from them, and carried up into heaven;" and that the disciples, after witnessing the Ascension, "returned from Mount Olivet, which is from Jerusalem a sabbath-day's journey." It is asserted with reason, by those who impugn the tradition, that, as the top of the Mount of Olives is not above half way to Bethany, therefore, to suppose the Ascension to have taken place from thence, is to wrest the obvious meaning of Scripture for the purpose of supporting tradition. Is it conceivable, indeed, that, if the disciples meant to affirm that Jesus ascended from the very summit of the Mount of Olives,—the most conspicuous spot in all the neighbourhood of the city,—they would have made use of language so calculated to mislead their readers? The only supposition that can be plausibly urged in favour of the tradition is, that Bethany was a name not merely applied to the village at the foot of Mount Olivet, but extended to the district on the eastern side; that the disciples are also said to have returned from "the mount to Jerusalem." This, however, can at best but warrant the conclusion—in itself most probable—that the Ascension, a sight reserved for the apostles alone, took place in the neighbourhood of the village of Bethany, in some secluded spot upon the eastern side of the Mount; but it can never justify so far-fetched an inference, as that which places the scene of it on the conspicuous summit of the hill, in sight of all Jerusalem. To this monkish tendency, indeed, of associating the most prominent spots with scenes of the Bible narrative, the tradition, in all probability, owes its origin.

The minaret, the chief object on the hill-top, has been already alluded to. The dome, hardly less conspicuous, stands over a small circular building, enclosing the rock upon which the impression of the Saviour's foot is visible,—at least to those gifted with sufficient faith to perceive it.

The site of the village of Bethphage, repeatedly mentioned as being adjacent to Bethany, has often been an object of research. It is said in one passage, in the account of our Lord's triumphal entrance, " when they drew near to Jerusalem, and had come to Bethphage, to the Mount of Olives,"—nearer apparently to the city than Bethany. No village answering to the situation is at present standing, but there are numerous traces about the hill which may serve to indicate its site. Dr. Olin thinks he has discovered it in a spot, a little more than a quarter of a mile nearly north from Bethany, where he found a large reservoir not used at present, lined with cement, and covered with an arch, with several foundations for houses, and heaps of stone and rubbish. Other traces of a similar nature were pointed out to me by Dr. Barclay, at a spot not very far distant from the top of the Mount of Olives, which perhaps has a better claim to be considered the genuine site.

One of the earliest notices of the buildings on the Mount of Olives is that of Arculf, who visited Jerusalem A.D. 700. He tells us, that on the highest point of Olivet, where our Lord ascended into heaven, is a large round church, having around it three vaulted porticoes. The inner apartment is not vaulted and covered, because of the passage of our Lord's body, but it has an altar on the east side, covered with a narrow roof. On the ground in the midst of it are to be seen the last prints, *in the dust*, of our Lord's feet; and the roof appears open above, where he ascended; and although the earth is daily carried away by believers, yet still it *remains as before, and retains the same impression of the feet.* Near this is a brazen wheel, as high as a man's neck, having an entrance towards the west, with a great lamp hanging above it on a pulley, and burning night and day. In the western part of the same church are eight windows; and eight lamps, hanging by cords opposite them, cast their light through the glass as far as Jerusalem, striking the hearts of the beholders with a mixture of joy and divine fear. Every year, on the day of the Ascension, when mass is ended, a strong blast of wind comes down, and casts to the ground all who are in the church. All that night lanterns are kept burning there, so that the mountain appears not only lighted up, but actually on fire, and all that side of the city is illuminated by it." Willibald, A.D. 723, mentions the open roof, and adds, in the middle of the church is a square receptacle, beautifully sculptured in brass, on the spot of the Ascension; and there is a small lamp in a glass case, closed on every side, that the lamp may burn always, in rain or fair weather. In Mandeville's day, the footprints of our Lord's feet in the *dust* were metamorphosed into the impression of *one* foot upon the *rock.*

After looking carefully around for the best point of view for exhibiting what is incomparably of more interest than anything else at Jerusalem,—the scenery of the New Testament narrative,—we found that none was so good as that from the roof of the old tower; and setting up there a camera obscura in Dr. B.'s possession, it was transferred to paper with extreme care, and afterwards compared with a photograph taken from the side of the hill, but on a less advantageous site. Nothing, of course, could exceed the minuteness of this latter; but it had the disadvantage that, under a strong light, there was no relief in the detail, and it was sometimes difficult to distinguish the more important buildings from the mass of inferior ones by which they were surrounded; so that to one not already acquainted with the place, the effect was somewhat confused and unintelligible. Representations of Jerusalem from the Mount of Olives are very numerous; yet I had never before seen one in which the hill itself was embraced, nor, till I visited my friend's tower, was I ever aware that it could be.

From this spot, which it should be borne in mind is on the *northern* side of the Mount, the conspicuous feature is its central and principal slope, crowned with the old Mosque and ruinous Church of the Ascension, before alluded to. Half-way down is the Chapel of the Prediction, as it is called, on a rocky knoll, on which, according to tradition, Jesus sat with his disciples when, exactly opposite to the Temple in all the pride of its stupendous masonry and portico resplendent with gold, he uttered the awful prophecy of its impending destruction; and certainly no spot appears more conformable to probability. Following down the hill-side to its base, just below an old Arab tower, similar to that from which the view is taken, appears the eight venerable olive-trees of the Garden of Gethsemane, enclosed within a high wall; and here again, if no exact certainty can be arrived at, we may reasonably presume that either at this spot, or within a very short distance, occurred the awful scenes of that night of agony which witnessed the betrayal of Jesus. The deep shades and caverns with which the bed of the valley is here filled, were also, in all probability, those to which he was accustomed to retire from the city, to converse with his disciples, and commune with his Father. The spot still retains much of the same character, abounding with gardens enclosed within low stone walls.

One of the most remarkable of these caverns, increased and shaped out by the hand of man, is seen in the view, close on the right of the Garden of Gethsemane. A flight of steps descends into an open court, surrounded with rocky walls, at the end of which is a singularly picturesque gothic façade (concealed in the drawing). Within this is a cavern, converted into a chapel richly adorned—the rock which appears in the view—traditionally called the Tomb of the Virgin; but it is very improbable that so extensive and costly an excavation should have been appropriated as the resting-place of the meek mother of Jesus, who lived and died in poverty and obscurity. The chapel, however, is sought by the pilgrims with a devotion, perhaps, greater than that paid to almost any other spot about Jerusalem.

Along that steep and rugged path winding up from the Garden of Gethsemane to St. Stephen's Gate, must have passed the procession conveying Jesus by torchlight to the house of the High Priest on the night of his betrayal,—at least if, as is hardly to be doubted, the Gate of St. Stephen stands on or near an ancient one, or unless the city wall at that time came down to the valley of the Kidron, and enclosed the whole hill on which the Temple stood.

After glancing at these places on the hill and in the valley of Jehoshaphat, a page may be devoted to the explanation of the rest of this panoramic view. The first object seen in the distance on the left, is the "Frank Mountain," as it is called; a conical hill not far from Bethlehem, in which stood a strong fortress, built and occupied by the Crusaders. Bethlehem itself is concealed by intervening hills, but the Convent of Mar Elyas, halfway to it from Jerusalem, is visible at the extremity of the Plain of Rephaim. Approaching the city, a solitary tree and mass of ruins are conspicuous on the top of a rocky hill, the base of which sinks down into the deep and trench-like valley of Hinnom, honeycombed with tombs and caves. This, according to tradition, is the tree on which Judas hanged himself; the ruins, those of the house of the high-priest Annas; and the hill, that of "Evil Counsel," from the plan laid between them to betray Jesus. The next object, outside the walls, is the long slope of Zion, "ploughed like a field," and dotted with olives, with the traditional Tomb of David, all which was formerly within the limits of the city. Within its bounds, near the corner, are the long white walls, and ground, and palatial buildings of the

Armenian convent, surmounting the dirty and wretched quarter of the Jews. To the right of that are the massive towers of the citadel; and under them, a white gothic edifice—the new English Church in Zion. Lower down, nearly in the centre of the modern city, and in a spot which certainly seems as though it never could have been without the ancient one, are the swelling domes and heavy massive tower of the Holy Sepulchre, and two adjoining minarets. Below this the ground sinks down into a hollow, in the centre of which is the Damascus Gate; and it rises on the opposite side into the hilly quarter, believed formerly to have been Bezetha, which occupies the angle as far as St. Stephen's Gate.

If we look to the high ridge just without the city on the north, beginning at a conspicuous Terebinth-tree at its north-west angle, we may trace the line of the third wall of the ancient city as far as a small Mahommedan tomb, whence it declined into the olive-ground below, and so swept the ridge of the upper valley of Jehoshaphat, till it joined the old wall of the valley of the Kidron; but whether this was on the ridge above, or, as some have suggested, in the valley below, is uncertain. Such an expression might well apply to either.

Still beyond this former limit of the city to the north, rises a high bleak ridge, the Scopus, where Titus first caught sight of the splendid city it was his predestined task to destroy. Here he first encamped, and hence directed his attack against the third or outer wall. In the extreme distance is a bold hill, crowned with a mosque, said to be built over the bones of Samuel.

It remains only to notice the central, and next to Olivet and Gethsemane, the most interesting portion of the view, namely, the great platform of Mount Moriah. It will at once appear, that this is the lower part of a long, rocky, tongue-like slope, descending from the high land on the north into the depths of the valley of Jehoshaphat. If we begin at St. Stephen's

Gate, a little to the left appears the northern wall of the area, above the deep trench separating it from the hill of Bezetha, but not visible in our drawing. A cluster of buildings and a minaret mark the north-west angle. These are at present the Governor's official residence. They stand on a scarped rock, as I have been repeatedly informed; and from this point the rocky surface of the interior, also scarped and bevelled, slopes downward toward the centre, approached through gates and studded with fountains.

This centre is occupied by the immense marble platform, on which stands the octangular Mosque of Omar, with its beautiful dome. To the left of this, resting on the extremity of the enclosure, is the long low roof of the Mosque el Aksa, with its graceful portico of seven gothic arches. At the south-east angle, above the remarkable masonry, is seen the roof of the Chapel of Sidni Issa, or our Lord Jesus, through which is a descent into the vaults which extend beneath this southern portion of the area, though precisely how far has never clearly been ascertained.

Then comes the most conspicuous object—the long extended wall, with its traces of ancient stone-work, and near its centre the "Golden Gate," walled up, but not for ever. Outside this wall are the white tombstones of the Turkish cemetery, and on the opposite side of the deep valley, the Burial-place of the Jews, with the "Tomb of Absalom," and rugged cliffs of the village of Siloam.

One question, we think, cannot but arise in looking at this hill of Moriah, namely, whether the line of wall, as we now see it, was the sole defence of the city upon this side, or whether it was enclosed by a second, which descended lower down towards the valley. Josephus, indeed, says that the city had but one wall where protected by impassable valleys, but it is difficult to ascertain his precise meaning. At the present day, steep as is the valley of Jehoshaphat, there is still abundant level space on the top to establish a point of attack. Probably, however, the immense strength of the Temple wall, formerly much higher, of which the base is no doubt buried in soil and rubbish, which may also have accumulated on the side of the hill, formerly more abrupt than now, would have proved too much for any means of attack before the invention of artillery. Still there is some uncertainty as to the solution of this question.

One of our principal amusements on the Mount of Olives was to look down upon the enclosure of the Mosque with a telescope, so powerful, that it not only showed with greater distinctness those objects already visible with the naked eye, but revealed a multitude of particulars which the latter at this distance was quite unable to discern. Often, for instance, when the area has appeared to be almost, if not altogether forsaken, an application of the optic tube showed numerous groups of figures, principally females, sitting in the shadow of the building, or that of the elegant Dome of the Chain, standing in front of it, which seemed a particularly favourite place of resort and gossiping on a warm afternoon. We could make out the varied costumes of the dervishes and others, which to the eye appeared so many dark specks, and also see people drawing water at the different fountains scattered over the surface of the area. Every detail of the building itself could be made out with the utmost clearness, even to the many-coloured pillars of the arabesque paneling with which the sides are encrusted. The beautiful pulpit near one of the south gates of the platform—a perfect gem of Arabian art—was a favourite object of examination. Distance, in short, seemed quite annihilated; and, seated at our ease, we were enabled to enjoy the beauties of the enclosure, almost as much as if privileged to wander freely about it.

Sketching by means of a telescope may not be considered a very legitimate or satisfactory operation; but the picturesque beauty of the central group of objects tempted me, nevertheless, to an attempt of the kind, which may serve to explain more clearly what is necessarily on a very small scale in the general panorama.

The foreground of the sketch is occupied by part of the grassy level of the area, and a few of the olive-trees, which, with majestic planes and cypresses, so beautifully diversify its surface, and give a character of union of art with nature almost peculiar to Turkish religious enclosures. The eastern gate, affording access to the great marble platform, is a prominent object. Part of this has been blocked up, either for support or some other reason, which greatly detracts from its architectural beauty. The stairs of this gate are called the Steps of Borak, the celestial horse on which the prophet ascended to heaven. Behind this is seen the Dome of the Chain, a most elegant little building, beneath which are seated groups of Turkish women in voluminous white wrappers, their faces covered with muslin handkerchiefs.

The Dome of the Chain, we are informed by Mejir-ed-Din, was built, like the great Mosque, by Abd-el-Melik-Ibn Merwan, and was so beautiful that it served as a model for that of the Sakhrah; but this can hardly be, for the two Domes are of different shapes. He tell us, also, that according to tradition, the prophet, on his nocturnal journey, here saw the Houris of Paradise.

Behind rises the Mosque itself, the exterior of which is encrusted with coloured marble and mosaic, in arabesque patterns of great variety and beauty.

The minaret rising to the left of the Mosque was erected, as Mejir-ed-Din informs us, by Tunguz, prefect of Syria, when he built the celebrated school at the side of the Gate of the Chain. It is revered by the most eminent Muezzins, and gives the direction to the others in announcing prayer. It stands near Bab-es-Salsala, or the Gate of the Chain, which opens into the Street of David.

Indeed, almost every rood of this sacred hill, which was the object of pilgrimage long before the Church of the Holy Sepulchre was built, has been encrusted with traditions, the object of which was to bring home to the imagination of the pilgrim every detail of the sacred narrative, and produce the most vivid feeling of reality. The spot where stood the two men who said, "Men of Galilee, why stand ye gazing up into heaven?" was marked by two columns, and an altar of St. Mary.

About a stone's throw from that place, Sœwulf tells us, is the spot where, according to the Assyrians, our Lord wrote the Lord's Prayer with his own fingers on marble; and there a very beautiful church was built, since destroyed by the Pagans Mandeville speaks of the same place as having "a chapel, in which is the stone on which our Lord sat when he preached the Eight Blessings; and there he taught his disciples the Paternoster, and wrote with his finger on a stone." He speaks, too, of "the place where our Lady appeared to St. Thomas the apostle after her assumption, and gave him her girdle. And very near it is the stone on which our Lord often sat when he preached; and upon that same shall he sit at the day of doom—as he said himself."

Arculf says, that "in the same valley, not far from the Church of St. Mary, is shown the Tower of Jehoshaphat, in which his tomb is seen." Of this worthy, Mandeville gives us the following curious account:—" This Jehoshaphat was a king of that country, and was converted by a hermit, and did much good. Adjoining to this little tower, on the right, is a separate chamber cut out of the rock of Mount Olivet, containing two hollow sepulchres—one, that of the ancient, Simeon the Just, who held the child Jesus in the Temple, and prophesied of him; the other, of Joseph the husband of Mary. On the south of Mount Olivet there is a cave not far from the Church of St. Mary, on an eminence looking towards the Valley of Jehoshaphat, in which are two very deep pits. One of these extends under the mountain to a vast depth, the other is sunk down straight from the pavement of the cavern, and is said to be of great extent. These pits are always closed above." Tradition has been busy here, too; for he adds, " In this cavern are four stone tables; one near the entrance is that of our Lord Jesus, and who, doubtless, rested himself here while his twelve disciples sat at the other tables."

Arculf speaks of the "round Church of St. Mary, divided into two stories by slabs of stone. In the upper part are four altars; on the eastern side below there is another; and, to the right of it, an empty tomb of stone, in which the Virgin Mary is said to have been buried; but who moved her body, or when this took place, no one can say. On entering this chamber you see, on the right hand side, a stone inserted in the wall on which Christ knelt on the night on which he was betrayed, *and the marks of his knees are still seen in the stone, as if it had been as soft as wax.*" Willibald solves the mystery hanging over the disappearance of the Virgin's body, by telling us the story he no doubt received on the spot himself, that "St. Mary expired in the middle of Jerusalem, in the place called St. Sion; and as the twelve apostles were carrying her body, the angels came and took her from their hands, and carried her to Paradise;" adding, that "the church is called after St. Mary, not because her body rests there, but in memory of it."

Not satisfied with establishing the general identity of Gethsemane, early tradition could rest contented with nothing less than pointing out the precise locality of every incident connected with it. Willibald, indeed, mentions "a church where our Lord prayed before his passion, and said to his disciples, 'Watch and pray, that ye enter not into temptation.'" Sœwulf speaks "of a certain oratory where our Lord dismissed Peter, James, and John, saying, 'Tarry ye here, and watch with me;' and going forward, he fell on his face and prayed, and came to his disciples, and found them sleeping. The places are still visible where the disciples slept, apart from each other. A little below, on Mount Olivet, is an oratory in the place where our Lord prayed, as we read in the passion; 'And being withdrawn from them about a stone's cast, and being in an agony, he prayed more earnestly, and his sweat was as it were great drops of blood falling down to the ground.'" Mandeville speaks of both chapels, adding of the one just named, that "in the rock we still see the mark of the fingers of our Lord's hand, when he put them on the rock when the Jews would have taken him." Maundrell mentions "a flat arched ledge of rock, reputed to be the place where Peter, James, and John fell asleep, during the agony of our Lord," but the chapel in his day was gone; and "a grotto"—that never-failing resource in Palestine—" is said to be the place in which Christ underwent that bitter part of his passion. About eight paces," he adds, "from the place where the apostles slept is a small shred of ground, twelve yards long and one broad, supposed to be the very path on which the traitor Judas walked up to Christ, saying, 'Hail, Master! and kissed him.' This narrow path is separated by a wall, out of the midst of a garden, as a *terra damnata*, a work the more remarkable as being done by Turks, who, as well as Christians, detest the very ground on which was acted such infamous treachery."

The door was closed at the time I passed, and not having a subsequent opportunity of visiting the place, I avail myself of a few notes by a friend who was more fortunate. "The monk (who acts as guardian of the enclosure) was now at his post, and a good-tempered looking Greek was also there, in whose company

I entered the garden. We formed a very sociable trio, as both the Greek and the Latin monks spoke Italian. The former told me a legend of Theodosius and the Patriarch carrying away earth from the Garden of Gethsemane, which dropped blood in his hand. I was glad to find that the old Franciscan repudiated the exactitude with which it was attempted to point out the precise spots of the events of the Gospel narrative, and thought the destruction of Jerusalem quite sufficient to preclude such knowledge..... The old man gave me a rose, as a memorial of the garden, from which I also brought a sprig of patriarchal olive. He smiled incredulously as he pointed out the spot where Judas betrayed our Lord with a kiss, and the dormitory of the three somnolent disciples. . . . I parted from the Franciscan with an invitation to renew my visit any time during my stay in Jerusalem, and, after taking coffee with my Greek friend, re-entered the city."

Before leaving the Mount of Olives, we must not omit to give some representations (furnished by Miss Barclay) of the very singular Tombs of the Prophets, the entrance to which is between

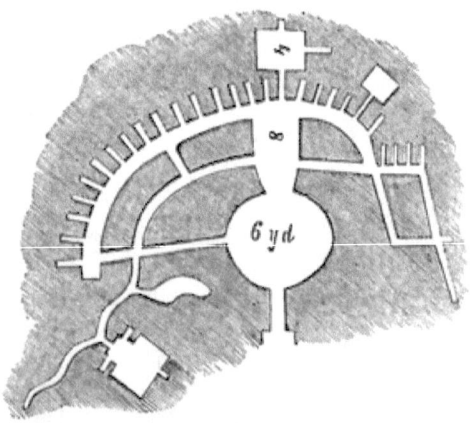

the Church of the Ascension and the Jewish burial-ground. The plan will show the intricate and puzzling nature of these rock-hewn sepulchres, which have puzzled the antiquaries beyond any other at Jerusalem. Some have even supposed them to have been connected with the idolatrous worship of Baal.

In company with a friend, I set out one afternoon from the Mount of Olives, to retrace the course of the Valley of Jehoshaphat, as far as its junction with that of Hinnom. On arriving at the foot of the hill, I was struck with the alteration made in the Garden of Gethsemane. At the period of my first visit, the eight olive-trees, traditionally so regarded, were easily accessible, standing on a plot of ground, surrounded only by a low stone fence. But since that time the monks have enclosed these venerated objects of pilgrimage within a high and solid wall; nor is this enough, but they have converted the spot into a trim, neat garden, full of flower-beds, thereby entirely destroying that wild and solitary character which gave such effect to the tradition. It must in justice be added, that they have thereby probably done much to preserve the trees, which formerly lay at the mercy of everybody who chose to tear off the bark, or cut down the branches.

Pacing slowly down the arid valley, we soon arrived at the Tomb of Absalom, which, with the surrounding rocks, the bridge over the Kidron, and the path leading steeply up the slope of Moriah, overhung by the south-east angle of the Temple with its ancient masonry, with the rugged cliffs of the village of Siloam winding out below, form one of the best known and most characteristic pictures about Jerusalem. This monument is a huge

POOL OF THE VIRGIN.

monolith, carved out of the rocky hill-side, the upper portion being afterwards built up. It certainly cannot challenge the praise of classical simplicity; and in its present ruinous condition, beautifully tinted as it is by weather stains, and adorned with the weeds and flowers that have taken root in its fissures and cracks, it is a more interesting object than it could have been in its more palmy days. The use of the classical orders would seem to indicate it as of the Herodian, or later period of Jewish architecture.

Pursuing our way down the Valley of the Kidron, we skirted the burial-ground of the Jews, passing a funeral group assembled around a newly-dug grave. This most melancholy cemetery is on the unenclosed and rugged slope of the valley, without a single tuft of verdure to relieve its aridity, or a tree to overshadow its crowded gravestones; yet no resting-place for their bones is so earnestly desired or so deeply venerated by the Jews as this,—sunk, as it is, under the shadow of the Temple, which towers above the opposite steep slope of the valley, and besides traditionally regarded as the chosen seat of that judgment which the Lord will one day execute in behalf of his oppressed people.

A short distance beyond the burial-ground, we descended into the bed of the valley, and reached the Fountain of the Virgin, or of Siloam, so called from the village or collection of hovels of that name, perched picturesquely among the tombs and cliffs on the opposite side of the valley. The rays of the sun poured down into the arid valley, and were reflected from its heated sides with such fervency, that we were glad to descend the upper flight of steps which leads down to the fountain, and to seek shelter in the cool, moist shadow of its overhanging arch. This is one of the most striking bits—to use an artistic phrase—anywhere about the city, as the illustration will partly show. At the landing of the upper steps, worn by the footfall of ages, we find ourselves, as it were, at the mouth of a mysterious-looking cavern, down into the jaws of which dives a second and much narrower flight of steps.

overhung with rocky projections, at the foot of which is found the spring. The women from the neighbouring village, ascending and descending, poising their water-jars upon their erect and often graceful figures,—with the groups of chance wayfarers, who come thither to seek refreshment for themselves and their horses, who are watered at a trough above,—add highly to the picturesque character of the spot.

Mejir-ed-Din, in his Arabian account of Jerusalem, gives a curious old tradition connected with this well, which he calls "the Fountain of Accused Women," to the effect that women accused of adultery came here and drank the water harmlessly if innocent, but with deadly effect if guilty. When Miryam (the Virgin Mary) was found with child and accused, she was submitted to this ordeal, and thus proved guiltless. She then prayed that this water might never harm any faithful woman; and from that day the fountain disappeared.

This last clause may perhaps allude to the well-known fact, that the water of this fountain ebbs and flows, the reason of which has never been fully ascertained. It is supposed to be supplied by an underground passage from the Temple area above, and to be dependent on some cistern or spring, which may vary in the supply of water. That there is a channel cut in the rock from hence to the Pool of Siloam, was proved by the enterprise of Dr. Robinson and Smith, who entering alternately at both ends, sometimes walking upright, at others bending on their knees, and in some cases creeping prone like serpents, at length succeeded in threading its entire length. Dr. R. remarks, with evident reason, that the purpose of such a work seems incomprehensible, unless the advantages of a fortified city are taken into account. Yet it seems very doubtful whether a spot in the level valley was included within the wall, unless we identify this with the "Pool of Solomon," by which Josephus tells us the lane passed between Zion and the Temple.

On leaving the Fountain of the Virgin, and directing our steps

towards the Pool of Siloam, we follow a stony path down the valley, here overhung on the right by the ridge on which formerly stood the quarter of Ophel, and on the left by the tombs and village of Siloam, and thus shortly reach the termination of the Valley of Jehoshaphat, at the point of its junction with the Valley of Hinnom.

Just above the dry pool, converted into a garden, is a very curious old tree, said to mark the scene of Isaiah's martyrdom; and, however dubious may be the tradition, yet, as a well-known object, and one yet, so far as I know, not hitherto engraved, perhaps a representation of it may not be uninteresting. Its roots are protected by a mass of stone-work, filled up with earth, and its ancient boughs, not "bald with dry antiquity," but still putting forth a considerable mass of foliage, are supported upon a pillar of stones. The tree stands precisely at the mouth of the Tyropeon, where it joins the Valley of Jehoshaphat, and the pathway leading up it to Mount Zion is seen on the left hand of the drawing. Immediately below, is the only *really verdant* spot about the city,—consisting of a few gardens of potherbs, irrigated by the water from the Pool of Siloam; and it is surprising what a magic there is even in this little patch of greenness in the desert of dust, rock, and sterility amidst which it is embedded. It is supposed to occupy the site of the "King's Gardens" in the days of Solomon.

This is quite a haunt of the neighbouring peasants; and the women and children are often very troublesome, pestering the traveller for "baksheesh" with a pertinacity that will accept no refusal. It was my fate to be thus surrounded, while drawing, by a group of black-eyed girls, some of whose faces, had they but been washed, might really have been considered handsome, or at all events expressive. Some of them carried babies, of which, juvenile as was their appearance, they were most probably the mothers; and, laughing all the while, studiously thrust the tattered clothing of their dirty infants into my very eyes, to create a feeling of sympathy. Annoyed at the interruption, I took at first no notice of them; whereupon they resorted to the most insinuating artifices,—calling me, in Arabic, "worthy Frank," patting me on the shoulder, ay, and even chucking me under the chin. I distributed two or three piastres among them, but this only served to draw down upon me a fresh set, until I suddenly bethought me of a very simple way to get rid of my persecutors. Fixing my eyes seriously upon one of the foremost girls, and then at my sketch-book, I pretended to be copying her lineaments, and thence glancing round at another, repeated the same manœuvre. No sooner was my design perceived than it was comical to mark the expression of alarm that came gradually over their countenances, at what they evidently considered a magical operation; and stealing off one by one, in a very few moments they left me to finish my sketch without any further interruption.

We now descended into the little corn-covered hollow at the junction of the two Valleys of Hinnom and Jehoshaphat, in the midst of which, almost buried amongst the surrounding hills, rocky and sterile, is the *Bir Eyub*, or Well of Job, as it is called by the natives,—the En Rogel of the Old Testament. It consists of a fountain, an arched chamber, a tank, and several drinking troughs. I climbed to the mouth of the well, which, according to Robinson, is 125 feet in depth, and drank from an old leathern bucket, worked up and down by a coil of rope drawn over a beam suspended for the purpose, bestowing a small baksheesh upon the Arab who drew for me. The quality of the water seemed to me to be far better than that of Siloam, and is highly esteemed in the city, an immense quantity being sent up daily on donkeys. There is a constant supply, and in rainy weather the surplus waters run off, and form a stream down the Valley of the Kidron.

This spot is chosen by the peasants of Siloam as a threshing-floor for the grain which they collect in the neighbourhood. The

mode of treading out the corn, as alluded to in Scripture, is represented in the engraving. Several oxen, being yoked abreast, revolve in a circle on a hard and level place chosen for the purpose, guided by an Arab armed with a stick, while another, with a rude sort of pitchfork, is occupied in tossing aside the straw. These rural occupations, with the groups of peasants seated among the corn, the ruined well, and bare rocky hills thinly dotted with olive-trees, composed a picture very characteristic of Palestine.

It would appear that this area, watered doubly by the irrigation from Siloam and from this well, and still the most fertile about the city, was originally the site of the " King's Gardens," where Adonijah gave a feast to his friends to engage them in his treasonable conspiracy.

The well appears to have been filled up and lost, and again reopened more than once, according to a story quoted by Mr. Williams from the continuator of William of Tyre. He says, that in the first year of King Baldwin IV., A.D. 1182, during a terrible drought in Jerusalem, a benevolent inhabitant, one Germanus, had supplied the thirsty inhabitants from some private reservoirs. These becoming exhausted, he bethought himself of an old well, said to exist near the Fountain of Siloam, but then filled up. After diligent research, he lighted upon the true spot, had the well cleared out, and erected a draw-wheel, with stone troughs, as we find them at the present day. He then employed men and horses to draw the water, and carry it up to the city above. On the approach of the Saracens it was again filled up, but afterwards reopened; and at the present day it forms one of the chief supplies of the city, a constant train of donkeys ascending and descending during the whole day.

From the threshing floor at En Rogel, we clambered by a steep pathway up to the angle of the Valley of Hinnom, the southern side of which is everywhere carved into sepulchres, the necropolis of the opposite Mount Zion. The rock is perfectly honeycombed with these excavations, which rise picturesquely one above another like those of Petra, connected by winding stairs. None of them display any exterior elegance or ornament, but considerable variety of style; some being square-headed, others arched, and others again pointed thus ∧, excavated at different periods of Jewish history. We have selected a characteristic group cut in the rock, overhanging the trench-like glen below, shaded by enormous fig-trees. The rugged slope of Mount Zion is seen on the other side, broken into terraces, along one of which not improbably ran the ancient first wall, if, as many suppose, it descended to the valley in order to enclose the Pools of Siloam and the Virgin.

On the brow of the precipice, under a large tree, is seen part of the ruined charnel-house standing on the traditionary *Aceldama*, or Field of Blood. Dr. Robinson tells us, that the tradition which fixes it upon this spot is as old as the time of Jerome, and that it is mentioned by a succession of travellers down to the present day. It was formerly devoted to the burial of pilgrims, and a few bones are still to be descried at the bottom of the vault. It was from this spot, as he informs us, that the earth was carried which fills the area of the Campo Santo at Pisa.

Dr. Schultz, the late learned Prussian consul at Jerusalem, descended into this place by means of a ladder, and found it to be one of the old rock graves, a double sepulchral cave, with numerous niches for corpses. The front wall is propped up, to prevent it falling in, by two pillars of bevelled stones neatly executed, which Dr. S. supposes to be of the Jewish period, and he imagines it to be the sepulchre of Annas, father-in-law of Caiaphas. He observes, that " a stratum of white clay, still coated, identifies it with the ' Potter's Field' of Scripture." If this be so, it has since served its original purpose of a burial-ground for strangers; having been successively used for that purpose by the Syrian Greeks, the Hospitallers, Franciscans, Greeks, and Armenians.

Not only this building, but also many of the adjacent sepul-

chres, appear to have been used as receptacles for the remains of others than their original tenants. We entered one tomb in particular, which has acquired the title of the genuine Aceldama, though on what ground it is difficult to imagine. There is a steep descent to this tomb, which is of very peculiar and very picturesque design. Lighting our candles and creeping in, we found an excavated chamber with a coved ceiling, from which opened numerous small chambers, penetrating deep into the rock. In these are carved troughs, each large enough for the reception of a single corpse, but this has long been consumed or displaced; and the dim light of our candles fell upon a miscellaneous collection of bones and skulls, crammed wildly into these funeral vaults, apparently brought from some other place, and stowed here for convenience; but who were the original tenants of the tomb, or who displaced them, there is no inscription to explain.

From some traces of painting within one of the tombs, representing saints, it may be inferred that it was adopted either as a chapel or a sepulchre during the middle ages.

These sepulchres, in short, seem to have undergone the same vicissitudes as the city itself, and to have served as burial-places to men of different races and creeds.

A very curious coincidence is mentioned by Mr. Williams, viz. that one of these rock tombs, described by Dr. E. Clarke, as exactly answering the description of our Lord's sepulchre, had been three centuries before pointed out by Boniface, the superior of the Franciscan Convent, who "uncovered and recased" the Sacred Tomb, as being, in every respect, identical with it!—a curious conundrum certainly, but which, it is hardly necessary to observe, proves nothing.

Undoubtedly the most singular and interesting tomb yet discovered in Jerusalem or its neighbourhood, is one of which I am favoured with the following notice by Dr. Barclay, accompanied with a sketch by his accomplished daughter: "In rambling round the environs of the city, I discovered very extensive foundations and remains of an ancient city, the site of which is

called by the Arabs 'El Musahney.' It lies on the two declivities of a ravine, entering Wady Beit Hanina, and is distant about a mile from its mouth, and upwards of two miles from this city;

nearly midway between the Tombs of the Judges (of which a representation is here introduced) and a village called Shafat.

There are a few joints of marble columns of immense size; but what interested me much more than anything else, is one of its large tombs, whose solid walls of native limestone are laid off in the Jewish bevilled style, and much of it is in as perfect a state of preservation as if executed but yesterday. As it is a genuine Hebrew work, and entirely unknown (this was in 1853) to the inhabitants of Jerusalem, I send you the enclosed sketch; and thinking that you would like to know something of the internal

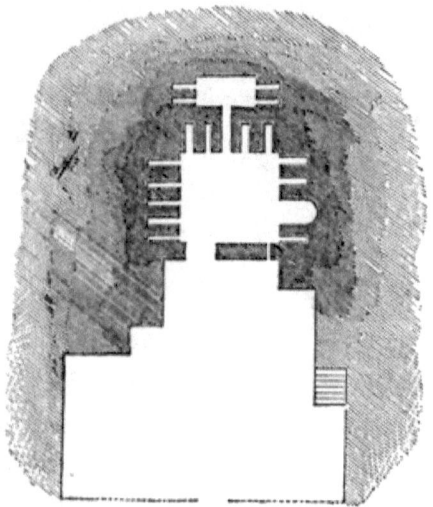

arrangements of a sepulchre, unequivocally Jewish, I subjoin also a plan of it, the correctness of which you may rely upon implicitly."

CHAPTER V.

The Haram Enclosure.

DIFFICULTY OF ENTRANCE—MR. TIPPING—ADVENTURE OF A FRIEND—MY OWN—RAMBLE ROUND THE EXTERIOR—PRINCIPAL OBJECTS WITHIN—VAULTS—THEORIES OF ROBINSON, WILLIAMS, AND FERGUSSON EXAMINED—PAPER BY MR. S. SHARPE.

I was in hopes that, during the years that had elapsed since my first visit to Jerusalem, the growing influence of the Franks, and possibly the increasing liberality of the Mussulmans, would have rendered access to the Haram more easy; but, though everybody agreed in saying that they hoped ere long all prohibition would be removed, it was admitted that, for the present moment, Moslem jealousy was as vigilant as ever, and that, unless disguised, it was quite impossible to get into the enclosure. This is a step certain, if discovered, to draw down the severest punishment upon the offender; nor has the consul any power to interfere, the offence being well known to be contrary to Mussulman law. The stimulus of intense curiosity, however, as well as scientific interest, has tempted more than one adventurer to brave these rules, and penetrate into the forbidden precincts; so that with the exception of a few interesting points not yet elucidated—such, for instance, as the vaults and cisterns supposed to exist somewhere beneath the surface of the enclosure, and the connexion of the water passages, at present so perplexing and mysterious—with these exceptions, the interior of the Haram may be said to be as well known as any other part of Jerusalem.

The remarkable adventure of Messrs. Catherwood, Bonomi, and Arundale, has been so fully described in the "Walks about Jerusalem," that it is only necessary to allude to it here. These gentlemen were enabled to survey every part of the area with the greatest minuteness, and the ground plan which I have seen drawn out from their measurements would cover the floor of a moderate-sized apartment. They also made plans of the substructions beneath the southern part of the area. No other traveller has been equally fortunate so as to add anything to the store of information thus obtained, unless it be Mr. Tipping, who availing himself of a window accidentally left open, crept into the subterranean vaults, and was enabled to make many interesting drawings of them before the matter was discovered.[1]

Not long before my own visit, I found, to my surprise, that a friend had succeeded in entering the enclosure, disguised as a Turk, and that through the agency of a dervish, who had bribed the guardian of the Mosque to keep his eyes fast closed on the occasion. Notwithstanding this, the adventure was very perilous; for the black keepers of the gates are exceedingly fanatical, and there is no telling what might be the result, were even an Englishman to fall into the hands of an enraged populace. The dervish, it should be observed, had himself proposed to my friend for the sake of a liberal baksheesh, to introduce him into the sacred precincts.

I have been favoured with an account of this gentleman's adventure, in which he writes:—"On returning to my lodgings, I found my dervish expecting me. He was to return at one, to fetch me for the attempt to visit the Mosque. Accordingly, a little after this hour, I issued out with him in Turkish costume. Taking my hand, he led me through some dark streets to the enclosure of the Haram. We passed unmolested through the

[1] Published in the new translation of Josephus by Dr. Traill.

sacred courts, and ascended the steps of the great platform. He pointed out to me a large cupola supported by columns, the traditional oratory of Abraham, Daniel, Solomon, and Jesus; and then, after peeping inside, led me into the interior of the Mosque of El Acksa. It was magnificently lighted, so that I lost nothing by the time at which I entered. There are six rows of massive columns, of different orders of architecture, leading up to the saharah, or sacred niche, which glows with red marble. I was placed behind a square pillar to make my devotions; and assuming the kneeling position which he dictated, escaped the suspicion of the keeper of the Mosque. In this position he left me some time; but I patiently awaited his return, and then stood with him under the vast marble dome, and gazed with delight at the slabs of red marble covering the walls. Before leaving the Mosque, I had to bestow a baksheesh on the doorkeeper, and did not give enough at first. I, therefore, had to feel in my pocket for more piastres; but luckily was not discovered in the attempt. We passed out of the Mosque by a different door, and passing again hurriedly through the enclosure, reached the gate, at which the guards gave us the *salam Allah koum*. The dervish returned the salute; I prudently held my peace. We reached my lodgings in safety, and the dervish took my hand, and put it to his heart to let me feel its palpitations. As he had not showed me all he promised, we agreed to deduct some of his fees; but still, as his terror and danger were great, I gave him the larger part of the sum promised.

"I had another proposition," he adds, "from my quondam neighbour to repeat my visit to the Haram. He promised that I should now see all that had been omitted in my previous visit, for which he had made arrangements with the doorkeeper. Accordingly I again assumed Turkish attire, and accompanied him. We visited first the Tomb of David, a cupola supported by circular colonnades, and shading a pavement of variegated marble. Entering into the great Mosque of Omar, we were admitted within the iron railings, and walked twice round the wooden palisades, which enclose the limestone rock of Mount Moriah, supposed formerly to have been the centre of the Holy of Holies. It is a rude unpolished mass, not peaked, occupying a space of about 400 feet square. Below it is a chapel, or rather a cave, into which we descended by a flight of steps. This is the traditional praying place of Abraham, David, Solomon, and Jesus; and it is an object of great veneration to the Mussulman. At various points in the circuit of the saharah are shown a niche with a tinfoiled head, and filled by a marble slab, on which are Arabic inscriptions—this is called the Tomb of Ipsa; a mark in the rock worn smooth by kisses of pilgrims, said to be the indentation of the foot of the angel Gabriel; the print of the five toes of Mahommed, carefully secured behind iron railings; the Tomb of Solomon; a slab of green marble; and a certain hole into which my hand was inserted, but I know not its supposed virtue. Hasson has promised to inquire. The marble columns which encircle the saharah are magnificent, and the effect of these huge masses of marble, when seen by daylight, must be very gorgeous. The whole floor is likewise composed of marble. Of the dome I could not catch a sufficiently accurate view to enable me to describe it, as we had only a candle for our exploration; but I saw the supporting columns, mentioned by Catherwood. Leaving the great dome-covered saharah, we visited, on our return, the Bir Arruah, a circular excavation extremely deep, according to my companion, but not closed by a stone, so far as I could see or feel. It is a circular orifice in a wall of marble. We then passed the olive under which Abraham is said to have offered his son; and I plucked a branch of it as a trophy, repassed the gate, and returned to my lodgings."

To this successful attempt to enter the Mosque, I will now add an account of one attempted by myself, which, though it proved abortive, may amuse the reader, as showing that, in spite of the bigotry of the Mussulmans in general, individuals are always to be found, and often of high standing, who are willing, for the sake of a bribe, not only to smuggle the infidel into the holy places, but also, rather than fail, to violate the established proprieties and rooted prejudices of their countrymen.

The agent in this instance was a character common enough in comedies, viz. an intriguing servant, belonging to a friend, whose profession as *Hakim* brought him into contact with many of the better class of Moslems. By his contrivance a meeting was brought about, at a house upon the brow of Mount Zion looking out on the ruined bridge, with an old Turk, who, having been previously sounded, had expressed his willingness to undertake the job. On repairing to the spot, I found one of the finest looking old men I ever saw, with an open, benevolent countenance, and a long silvery beard, dressed in a turban and white robes, and looking the very impersonation of one of the patriarchs. After mutual salutations, the business was opened by my interpreter, and the best means of effecting it were canvassed with great earnestness. As I wore neither beard nor moustache, and, besides, had not been long enough in the country to get thoroughly bronzed, the old man at first proposed that I should be dressed as a Turkish woman, and walk behind him about the Mosque. This plan, however, had its objections, and on further reflection, he was struck with a most original idea, and certainly the last of which I should ever have thought. I was to come to his house after dark, apparently as a Hakim sent for to prescribe for his family, with the intriguing servant carrying a box of medicine before me, in order to lull suspicion. On arriving at his domicile, he would have a woman's costume all ready, in which I was to dress myself,—a disguise in which, no doubt, many more nefarious pranks have been played than I was about to commit. Having put on this feminine attire, I was then to accompany his wives to the Mosque, which would at that time be brilliantly illuminated, this being the season of the Ramadan. The only difficulty, he said, would be to talk over his women, but to persuade them into the scheme, he trusted to the efficacy of a certain five hundred piastres, which I promised to pay down as soon as we came back to his house, after the successful conclusion of the adventure.

I now returned home, and from the terrace of the hotel watched the red light fade off Mount Olivet, and heard the gun fired to give notice to all good Moslems that they might now lawfully eat their dinners. Darkness soon invested the city, relieved only by the brilliant stars, and the red glimmer of the lamps suspended on the tops of the minarets. As the time drew near when the servant was to come and fetch me, it now suddenly struck me that I had embarked in a rather hazardous affair, without anything to justify it but the mere desire of an adventure; since it would be impossible, muffled up in female attire, to examine the architectural peculiarities of the Mosque, even if the act of staring about would not of itself be enough to betray my disguise. In the event of discovery, there could hardly be a doubt that death by stoning, or some more horrible fate, would be the penalty inflicted upon me by the fanatic mob, doubly enraged at the violation of the sanctity of the place, and at the indecent manner in which it had been effected.

It was, then, with no little nervousness that I listened for the tap at the door which was to announce the messenger. About nine he made his appearance, informing me that the old man had succeeded in talking over his womankind, and that everything was in readiness. We then stole forth, the servant gravely preceding me, and carrying before him a travelling-box of medicines. This precaution was all but useless, for the streets were so dark that it was with difficulty we could grope our way; but here and there we came upon a group of Turks sitting out of doors, and smoking by the light of paper lanterns. The last of these was in the Via Dolorosa, near St. Anne's Church; and I thought I recognised among them the ugly visage of a lad who had thrown stones at me in the morning, for approaching too near the mosque, and who regarded me with a look of suspicion.

At length we reached the house of the old Turk. On stepping in, I was conducted with an air of mystery into an upper chamber, when the old Turk came forth and welcomed me. I could not but remark that, notwithstanding the confidence he had previously expressed, his countenance betrayed no little agitation. He uttered, from time to time, a deep sigh, stroked his long beard, and, looking up to heaven, muttered what I understood was a prayer for the happy success of the enterprise. In fact, he must have been conscious that, should a discovery take place, he would be certain to forfeit all consideration and character, even if subjected to no further punishment, which, however, would most probably be the case.

The articles of female dress intended for my disguise were now produced, and I was invited to put them on. The first difficulty occurred with the boots of yellow leather, in which the Turkish women waddle rather than walk about the streets. These were so small that it was impossible to get them on, and I had therefore to content myself with slipping my stockings into a pair of red shoes which only half covered them. My feet seemed alarmingly large and clumsy, and very likely to betray my real sex; but the Turk and servant said these would do. The next affair was to draw over my pantaloons a pair of female inexpressibles, which, though of very spacious width, turned out, like the boots, to be too small, scarcely reaching down to the ankles, which stood out in strong development. Their sole fastening was a pair of strings, intended to be drawn round the slender waist, and to rest upon the swelling hips of the fair owner; but from the want of any such support in my case, they threatened to slip bodily down upon the slightest movement. A dark veil was now put over my head, so as to entirely conceal the features, but through which I was enabled to see with tolerable clearness; and finally, a large white wrapper, but also too short, was thrown over me, completely enveloping all but the face. Although I fancied this disguise far from complete, the old man and the servant, after studying it attentively, and asking me to walk up and down, dropping my head a little, and affecting something of a female waddle, looked at one another with approving glances, and authoritatively pronounced it to be " taib."

The servant now explained to me the manner of proceeding. When the women were dressed, which would be in a few minutes, we were all to sally forth together, and enter the enclosure by the neighbouring gate. I was instructed to keep in the middle of the party, to do precisely as they did, and to be careful not to stare too much about me. We were to go first into the Mosque of Omar, which at that moment would be brilliantly lighted up, and from thence to that of El Aksa; returning, after a short stay, to the house, where I was then to count down the five hundred piastres which I had stipulated to give.

All was now ready, and I awaited the arrival of my female conductors with intense anxiety, not altogether unmingled with apprehension. To say truth, besides doubts as to my own successful deportment, I was not without misgivings as to the discretion of my companions, in a case where the slightest misconduct would involve the most serious consequences; and feared no less, than in case of alarm they would suddenly scatter about the enclosure, and leave me to get out of it as I could. My distrust was greatly increased when I heard much chattering without, and when the head of the chief lady was projected into the apartment, beckoning forth her husband, who followed her into an adjoining room. He returned in a moment, evidently much disconcerted, declaring that his wives would only consent to accompany me on previously receiving payment. Stroking his beard, he declared that he had himself no misgivings whatever, and trusted entirely to my honour, but that his wives were rebellious and would listen to no reason. I was doubly annoyed at this,—not only because it involved a personal affront, and displayed the avaricious eagerness of the women in a disgusting light, but also because it confirmed me in my distrust of their conduct. To pay them beforehand what was so evidently their only inducement to go with me, would deprive me of the sole check I might have upon their behaviour, and I firmly resolved not to surrender it. Producing the money, which I had brought with me, I declared that it should be paid down the very moment we returned, but that after the formal agreement which had been entered into, it was doubting my honour to insist upon receiving it beforehand. A spirited discussion now ensued, the women thrusting their heads into the room, and taking part in it. I found they were divided in opinion, and that it was the obstinacy of the chief lady which prevented the conclusion of the bargain. The poor old Turk seemed passive in their hands, and altogether it afforded a curious insight into the manifold tribulations besetting the possessor of many wives, proving that polygamy is to be regarded, as Byron says—

"Not only as a sin, but as a bore."

As the women still persisted in their demands, I at length got wearied, and throwing off the feminine garb in which I was half-suffocated, broke off all further negotiation. The servant resumed his lantern and medicine-chest, the old Turk preceded me into the street, and took leave with every demonstration of courtesy, and regret that the matter had come to so untoward an issue. The Haram was no doubt in a pretty state of combustion after our departure.

Although most points connected with the enclosure have been noticed in the "Walks," it may not be too much to take another ramble around and within the area, describing such of its more prominent objects as had previously escaped notice, as well as the theories that have been recently put forth upon the subject.

In tracing the external wall of the Haram, let us commence at its north-east angle, without St. Stephen's Gate. Here we have undoubtedly, in a corner projection, a considerable mass of the original masonry, though perhaps only a reconstruction, facing both north and east. This is continued along the lower lines of the wall, as far as the Golden Gate, on each side of which are several very massive stones. The gateway itself, now walled up, does not appear of such high antiquity, but seems rather stuck in afterwards; and the observation of Mr. Ferguson is worthy of notice, that it bears no marks of a defensive, but wholly of an ornamental character.

From the Golden Gate, the rest of the wall, as far as the south-east angle, shows no traces of what we shall venture to call, for the sake of distinctiveness, Jewish masonry, owing perhaps to the ground having here greatly accumulated; but it descends rapidly as we approach the corner, exposing a mass of stupendous stone-work, the base evidently buried in the earth, and rising almost to the top of the lofty wall. The lower courses, from their immense size and regularity, appear as if unchanged; but the upper are less regular, and there is in many places an appearance of reconstruction at a later age. But these peculiarities, together with the manner in which the smaller masonry is placed upon the larger, are better conveyed by the pencil than by the pen. It will be borne in mind that the lower part of the space within is occupied by arched vaults.

Proceeding now along the southern side, we continue to see traces, though less striking, of the same stone-work, till we come to three arches in the wall, which it is difficult to account for, unless we suppose them to be external indications of a gateway formerly leading through the vaulted arches up to the platform of the Mosque, which indeed appears to be the case. The next object is a gateway, externally resembling in style the Golden Gate, and, like that, now blocked up. Only a portion of this is visible, the rest being concealed by out-buildings. Through a grated window, formerly accessible, Mr. Tipping contrived to get access to the vaults within, and make drawings of the archway leading up beneath the Mosque El Aksa, described by Mr. Catherwood in the "Walks about Jerusalem," but of which Mr. T. has furnished us with a more detailed account in the notes to "Traill's Josephus."

It has been for some time an object of interest to discover, if possible, traces of the piers of the bridge, but the work is extremely difficult, on account of the rubbish and prickly pears which cover the site; and though Dr. Barclay has repeatedly endeavoured to get workmen to engage in the task, they have either declined or backed out from the business when about to commence. He has, however, been assured that the foundations in question are certainly there.

One discovery, however, made by the doctor in this neighbourhood, is of peculiar value, as adding to the evidence that the bridge and masonry really belonged to the old temple wall. "In rummaging," he says, "through the dark rooms at the south end of the Wailing Place, I discovered a huge portal of a gateway at the junction of Abu Seud's house with the temple wall, just beneath the present Mugaribah Gate. This lintel is seven feet by sixteen, as far as can be seen; the house of Abu Seud secluding the remainder from sight, so that I am unable to ascertain its total length. This gate is doubtless the second of the four exits from the western side of the ancient temple area."

Here our further progress along the wall of the Haram is abruptly brought to a close by its junction with that of the modern city. Supposing ourselves, however, on the opposite side of this obstruction, we find a continuation of several courses of the same massive masonry, as far as the south-west angle. We now follow the western wall, where we soon fall in with further interesting and remarkable traces of it. The first is the well known fragment of an arch projecting from the lower courses of the wall, supposed, with every appearance of reason, to be the starting point of the bridge described by Josephus as connecting the temple with Mount Zion, and of which a description has been already given in the "Walks."

Here, again, our investigation of the wall is stopped by a group of buildings which has been raised against it, but making a circuit round these obstructions, and descending a narrow lane, we shall find it again at the "Jews' Wailing Place," perhaps the most regular and best preserved portion of the whole enclosure now exposed to view. Beyond this point all possibility of tracing the wall is prevented by its being embedded in a mass of Arab houses and colleges abutting upon the Haram wall, which, besides, are inaccessible to the scrutiny of Europeans, though, from remarks by Mr. Catherwood, made during his survey, there can be no doubt that it partly exists all along this side to the north-west angle.

The paper inserted in "·Walks about Jerusalem," giving a general description of the interior of the Haram, the Mosques, and other objects, precludes the necessity of going into the subject with any great minuteness here. Still a few additional notices may not perhaps be superfluous on a matter of so much interest, accompanied as they are by a plan and sketches, furnished by the same kind friend to whom I was originally indebted.

In this plan the external boundary of the enclosure is laid down as in Mr. Catherwood's original survey, and not according to the pretended corrections, the value of which has been already tested.

Let us suppose the area thrown freely open to our inspection, and that we enter it by the gate, near the Pool of Bethesda. As we proceed along the northern line of the interior, we first pass the modern wall and minaret overhanging the pool, and which occupy the site of the ancient one, defending the temple on the north. Beyond this is a line of buildings forming schools and colleges, and the official residence of the governor, and standing most probably on the site of the old Fort Antonia. This position was laid down in the "Walks," nor can we see any reason to recede from it, notwithstanding other theories that have been put forth. The buildings stand partly on a scarped rock; and it is to be observed that the area itself is here rock, and slopes evidently downward for some distance towards the centre. This was observed a second time, and clearly shows that there can be no trace of any valley, such as Schultz supposes to have once run across the area. The façade of these buildings is a highly picturesque and curious specimen of Arabian architecture. The lofty and handsome minaret at the north-west corner was built, according to Mejir-ed-Din, in A.D. 1297-8, by an inspector of the religious foundations of Mecca, Medina, and Jerusalem.

One gate gives access to the area upon this side, by a dark passage running out of the Via Dolorosa, not far from St. Anne's Church.

In front of the governor's house stand out two or three of those pretty isolated fountains, or praying places, which, intermingled with trees, confer so beautiful a character upon the religious enclosures of the Moslems. That marked No. 2 upon the plan is called the "Dome of Solomon."

Retracing our steps to the north-east corner, and following the eastern side, the first object we meet, attached to the wall, is a small building, called the "Throne of Solomon."

The next object is the celebrated Golden Gate, an exterior view of which is to be found in the "Walks." The interior displays precisely the same architectural character.

This building is certainly an architectural and historical

puzzle. It cannot be, of course, one of the old temple gates, though its resemblance to that beneath the Aksa would seem to imply it; and its situation at once shows that it cannot be what Mr. Ferguson supposes; viz. the approach to the Church of

Constantine, which we are told opened on the market-place of the city. To what period can we then assign it? The most probable answer would be, to that of Hadrian, when he rebuilt the city; yet it is one, we confess, in which we have not much confidence.

The great platform, the Mosque of Omar, and the rock over which it is built, with the Dome of the Chain, have been fully described.

The only object which deserves an additional notice connected with the platform is the Mohammedan pulpit and staircase, close to the southern gate. This is an exquisite specimen of Arabian architecture, as may be judged of from the annexed engraving.

Ali Bey tells us that across this gate will be suspended the invisible balance, in which are to be weighed the actions of the just and of the unjust.

To the very interesting account of the interior of the Mosque of Omar (so called), given in the "Walks" by Mr. Catherwood, may be added a few other curious details.

Ali Bey gives a very interesting and correct account of the rock of the "Sakhara," and the Moslem traditions connected with it.

"The plane of the central circle is raised three feet above the plane of the surrounding naves, and is enclosed by a high and magnificent railing of iron gilt. This central circle encloses the sacred rock called El Sakhara Allah; it is the principal object of this superb edifice, and, generally speaking, of the Temple or Haram of Jerusalem.

"El Hadjira el Sakhara, or the Rock of Sakhara, rises from the earth upon a mean diameter of thirty-three feet, in form resembling the segment of a sphere. This surface is unequal, rugged, and in its natural state. Towards the north end there is a hollow, which tradition relates to have been formed by the Christians, who wanted to carry away that part of the rock which is wanting, but which then became invisible to the eyes of the infidels. The faithful believers afterwards found this part divided into two pieces, which are now in other parts of the Haram, and of which I shall treat hereafter.

"The Mussulman believes that the Sakhara Allah is the place of all others, except El Kaaba, or the House of God at Mecca, where the prayers of men are most acceptable to the Divinity. It is on this account that all the prophets, since the creation of the world to the time of the prophet Mohammed, have come to this spot to pray; and even now the prophets and angels come hither in invisible troops to make their prayers on the rock, exclusive of the ordinary guard of 70,000 angels, who perpetually surround it, and who are relieved every day.

"On the night when the prophet Mohammed was carried away

by the angel Gabriel, and transported in a moment through the air to Jerusalem, upon the mare called El Borak, which has the head and neck of a fine woman, as also a crown and wings, the prophet, leaving El Borak at the gate of the temple, came to offer up his prayer upon El Sakhara, with the other prophets and angels, who, having saluted him respectfully, yielded to him the place of honour.

"At the moment when the prophet stood upon El Sakhara, the rock, sensible of the happiness of bearing the holy burden, depressed itself, and, becoming like soft wax, received the print of his sacred foot upon the upper part, towards the south-west border. This print is now covered with a large sort of cage of gilt metal wire, worked in such a manner that the print cannot be seen on account of the darkness within, but it may be touched with the hand through a hole made on purpose. The believers, after having touched the print, proceed to sanctify themselves by passing the hand over the face and beard. In the interior of the rock is a cave, into which they descend by a staircase on the south-east side. There is a room forming an irregular square of about eighteen feet surface, and eight feet high in the middle. The roof is a natural irregular vault. In descending the staircase, there is upon the right at the bottom a little tablet of marble, bearing the name of El Makam Souloman, or the Place of Solomon. A similar one on the left is named El Makam Davoud, or the Place of David. A cavity or niche on the southwest side of the rock is called El Makam Ibrahim, or the Place of Abraham. A similar circular concave step, at the north-west angle, is named El Makam Djibrila, or the Place of Gabriel; and a sort of table of stone, at the north-east angle, is called El Makam Hodei, or the Place of Elias.

"In the roof of the room, exactly in the middle, there is an aperture, almost cylindrical, through the whole thickness of the rock, about three feet in diameter. It is called the Place of the Prophet.

"The rock is surrounded by a wooden fence, about a leaning height; and above, at an elevation of about five or six feet, is a canopy of red and green silk, in alternate stripes, suspended over the whole breadth of the rock by pillars and columns.

"From what I could discover, particularly in the inside of the cave, the rock seemed to be composed of a reddish white marble.

"Near this place, on the north side, may be discovered in the pavement a piece of very fine waved green marble, about fifteen inches square, fastened down by four or five gilt nails. This, they say, is the Door of Paradise; several holes in the marble indicate it to have been fastened formerly by a great number of nails, which are supposed to have been pulled out by the devil, when he wished to enter Paradise, and was prevented by not being able to pull out the nails which remain."

Every part of the sacred enclosure is, besides the solemn facts of history, the subject of innumerable traditions, Jewish, Christian, and Mohammedan. The Moslems, who extend to the legends of other religions the same ready credulity they display towards their own, have inlaid this whole area with a complete Mosaic work of marvellous traditions, in which Old Testament Saints, the Saviour and Mary, Mohammed, the angel Gabriel, the celestial horse Borak, and the valiant St. George, are all intermingled and confounded together. But the centre of all these marvels is the Sakhara. Mejir-ed-Din says, that the author of Messir-el-Ghoram relates, that he found in the commentary on the work Muta (a collection of traditions of the Imam Malek), on that verse of the Koran, "We sent water from heaven," that all the water on earth comes from the Sakhara; which is a marvel, because being itself without support on any side, it is supported only by Him who supports the heavens, which can only fall upon the earth by his permission. On the south side is the footprint of the prophet, when he mounted the celestial beast Borak for the nocturnal journey, which occasioned the rock to incline on this side out of respect. On the other side you see the prints of the fingers of the angels who supported the rock while it bowed. Beneath the rock is a cave, in which prayers are always heard. "When I would enter there, (continues the author of Messir-el-Ghoram,) I feared that it would sink down under the burden of my sins; but having seen that sinners, covered with all kinds of iniquity, entered, and came out safe and sound, I took courage to enter. I still hesitated, however; at last I entered, and was astounded to see the rock detached on all sides, and not joined to the earth." So writes the author of Messir-el-Ghoram; but it is a well-known fact among men, that this rock is suspended between heaven and earth. It is said that it remained so suspended until a pregnant woman, when she had entered under the rock, being terrified with this appearance, miscarried there. Then it was surrounded with the present building, to conceal the terrific marvels of the place. The Bir Arruah, or "Well of Souls," which descends from the centre of this redoubtable cavern, has been already noticed. Both Jews and Moslems, as well as Christians, regard this rock as connected with Solomon's Temple. When the Moslems were for awhile expelled, and the Crusaders obtained possession of the spot, they overlaid it, like other sacred places, with a mass of traditionary localities. Thus Sæwulf, who visited Jerusalem at that time, after identifying the Mosque with the Temple of Solomon, says: "In the middle is seen a large and high rock, hollowed beneath, in which was the Holy of Holies. In this place Solomon placed the ark of the covenant, having the manna, and the rod of Aaron, which flourished and budded there, and produced almonds, and the two tables of the Old Testament. Here our Lord Jesus Christ, wearied with the insolence of the Jews, was accustomed to repose; here was the place of confession, where his disciples confessed themselves to him; here the angel Gabriel appeared to Zacharias, saying, Thou shalt receive a child in thy old age; here Zacharias the son of Barachias was slain between the temple and the altar;" here (to abridge his description) was the offering of our Lord, and here he was found sitting in the midst of the doctors. The footmarks of Jesus, as well as those of Mohammed, were here to be seen in the rock, when he concealed himself, and went out from the Temple, lest the Jews should stone him; and finally, here the woman taken in adultery was brought before him for judgment. And, but that the reader has probably had enough, we might largely increase the list by quoting others from Mandeville.

North-west of the Mosque also, on the marble platform, are two places connected with the tradition of Mohammed's nocturnal journey. That nearest to the Mosque is called the Place of the Prophet, where he prayed with the angels and cherubim, and whence he ascended to heaven. Near this is the Dome of the Ascension, built A.D. 1199-1200, also regarded with deep veneration by pilgrims.

If we now cross from the marble platform to the western wall, and follow it to the south-west corner, we reach the chapel called the Sidna Jesa, or Cradle of Jesus, a subterranean oratory, and where it is said that Miryam, or Mary the mother of Jesus, performed her devotions; and here (says Mejir-ed-din) they recited the prayer of Jesus, when he ascended from the Mount of Olives. This tradition may not improbably have arisen in some way from Justinian's Church of St. Mary, either identical with the Aksa, or standing over this very site. On the level ground above, Dr. Barclay discovered traces of tesselated pavement, which may not improbably have belonged to it. From this chapel is the entrance to the subterranean vaults, extending under this part of the area.

Since the publication of the "Walks," these vaults have been explored by Mr. Tipping, who has given several very interesting drawings of them, in his illustrations to "Traill's Josephus." They serve entirely to confirm Mr. Catherwood's description, resembling in general the interior of the Golden Gate; but, as Mr. Tipping with reason imagines, bearing evident traces, in parts, of an antiquity coeval with that of the massive exterior stonework, and confirming the idea that these are, in the main, the work of Herod the Great, if not of older times.

The idea that these massive vaults, with the gateway leading up into the area, and the exterior stonework which encloses them, were, as Mr. Williams imagines, the works of the Emperor Justinian, may safely be dismissed, without the trouble of refutation. Indeed, Mr. Williams's friend and fellow-defender of the Sepulchre (Professor Willis) cannot but regard the vaults as having sustained the magnificent double cloister of the Temple, the work of Herod, which communicated by the bridge with the opposite brow of Mount Zion.

The exploration of these mysterious substructions appears, after all, to have been but partial. Mr. Catherwood found that further progress was stopped by walls that had been built for the purpose, or earth that had fallen in from the area above. We must, therefore, await the period—perhaps not far distant—when the whole area shall be thrown open to the scientific examination of Europeans. It may then not improbably appear that there are vast cisterns, supported, like those at Constantinople, on columns, with which are connected the numerous wells within and around the area,—the mysterious pools of the Virgin and Siloam,—with the whole system of those water-courses, as Tacitus describes them, " cavati sub terra," at the connexion of which we can at present but dimly guess. Perhaps some curious objects or valuable treasures may be disinterred from niches in which they may have been hidden by the priests, on the sack of the Temple, and the secret of which perished with their massacre.

These anticipations have been remarkably fulfilled, as will be seen by the following extracts from a letter received from Dr. Barclay, who, shortly after my return, had the singular good fortune to obtain free entry of the forbidden precincts of the Haram, like Mr. Catherwood, in capacity of an engineer:—

" *March* 1*st.* 1854.—After brooking various disappointments, delays, and difficulties, I have at last been gratified by the amplest opportunity of deliberately examining the Haram Enclosure; and when I assign as the cause of thus long delaying the completion of this communication, the employment of this rare opportunity, I am sure you will excuse this unavoidable delay. Being introduced into the Haram by the very gentlemanly Effendi appointed by the Sultan to superintend its reparation, and generally accompanied by him, or his courteous brother, my access has been almost unrestricted; but as yet I have only made five critical examinations, spending each time four or five hours, but I expect to continue my examinations almost *ad libitum*. Much of this time has been spent in making a complete plan of the sacred area; so that I have not yet made a minute examination of some of the most interesting points of inquiry."

"You were not altogether mistaken in your conjecture about the ground at which you were so intently looking through the telescope, from our old ruin on Olivet: a large extent of the surface a short distance north-west of Sidna Jesa is still paved with tessera *in situ*, just as the floor of Aksa is at present. How the British engineers could have committed such a blunder in surveying the south-west corner of the area is really matter of astonishment. I have not yet succeeded in entering beneath this corner; and I begin to think, contrary to the generally received opinion, that it contains no such pillars as those in the south-east corner, but is either composed of native rock entirely, or so nearly so that the necessary elevation was made, not by vaults and pillars, but simply filled up with coarse masonry,—at least the portion of it now occupied by the foundation of the Mosque, commonly called Abu Bekir, which once sustained a portion of the royal portico of the Temple. I tried, but in vain, to penetrate it through a partial opening in the wall under Aksa. No vacuity beneath is known to any of the keepers of the Haram; but I lay no peculiar stress upon this; for none of them were aware of any indication of a former gate, near Abu Seud's house. A very slight search, however, revealed it to my view on the interior as evidently as on the exterior; but apparently *faced* in Roman style, and patched somewhat in Turco-Saracenic fashion; so that the present opening is only eighteen or nineteen feet wide. But as this is a point at which no repairs are contemplated, I must not inspect it too curiously yet awhile, lest by so doing I should jeopardize my freedom of access; for all my movements are sedulously watched and jealously scrutinized. As soon as I hear from an individual in Beirut, in relation to some materials for the construction of water-raising apparatus, I shall explore a large bîr in the angle formed by 'Abu Bekir' Mosque, and that of the Mograbins; where I hope to ascertain something more decisive as to the substructions of the south-west corner. I was very forcibly reminded of the 'montes cavati sub terra' of Tacitus, in exploring a large reservoir in front of Aksa, east of the broad walk laid down in Catherwood's plan. It is indeed a beautiful subterranean lake, being the grand reservoir for the water brought from 'Solomon's Pools.' It is nearly fifty feet deep, and interspersed with little islands of rock, upon which similar-shaped tapering rock-work has been reared to support the ground above. Judging from the large number of wells with which my chart is dotted, a very large portion of the Haram ground must be cavernous. Even in the north-west corner, where the natural limestone rock constitutes the surface, there are several extensive tanks, but I am not aware of the existence of any other kind of vacuity in that quarter. I am very anxious to examine critically the indications of a passage leading northwards from the noble cave (under Omar), in the hope that it may prove to be the Herodian communication of which Josephus makes mention, between the Temple and the Tower of Antonia. This reminds me of an immense cavern under Bezetha Hill, that I have lately explored. It is entered from the little ridge of earth just east of the deep depression, (apparently an old tank from the Damascus Gate,) where the natural rock forms about half the height of the wall. It varies in width from twenty to one or two hundred yards, and extends about two hundred and twenty yards in the direction of the Seraglio, terminating in a deep pit, in which we found the most *cubical*-shaped head of a human skeleton that I have ever seen. Alas, poor Yorick! This immense skeleton is doubtless that of a too adventurous explorer, whose light perhaps became extinguished; or he may accidentally have fallen into this 'horrible pit.' The very idea made us shudder, and handle our lights very circumspectly, as we cautiously crept through these immense halls and passages."

We may here briefly examine a theory, which, from its startling character and the skill with which it is supported, has puzzled, though not convinced, even those best acquainted with the subject. Mr. Ferguson's argument is twofold : 1st, that the cave within the rock of the Mosque of Omar is the true sepulchre of Christ; 2d, that the building over it is not, as generally supposed, a Mohammedan Mosque, but the Round Church erected over the sepulchre by Constantine.

The first of these positions, it should be observed, is not necessarily connected with the second; since, admitting that this edifice was built by Constantine, it would by no means follow that he had lighted upon the true spot. Mr. Ferguson's argument in favour of its being the latter involves the highest degree of improbability. Even were his theory admitted, which it cannot be, that the Temple occupied merely the south-west angle of the present enclosure, its immediate neighbourhood must surely have been devoted to other purposes than that of public executions. Nor is it to be credited that one solitary tomb should have been found precisely on this spot, and on no other near; and that one devoted to the reception of a reputed malefactor. But no one who looks at the city for a moment can ever believe that this spot was without the city walls; since, instead of ranging along the brink of the valley—the only defensive line—it would have left all the summit of Moriah an open level for the operations of a besieging army; and it may well be said that such an idea could only have been seriously entertained by one who had never visited the spot.

The second position, viz. that this is really the Church built by Constantine, is chiefly based by Mr. Ferguson on the study of its *architecture*, a point on which he may be considered a more competent authority than any preceding writer on Jerusalem. He affirms that, notwithstanding the Saracenic dome and casing which have so long deceived the eye, the interior arrangements and details are obviously of the age of Constantine. This assertion is founded principally on a drawing of Mr. Arundale's, displaying the main aisle, in which the capitals are of a debased Corinthian, and the cornice of a corresponding style, the roof also being flat, and having no Saracenic type. This, indeed, has every appearance of being modern. Mr. Ferguson's assertion, however, that this Christian type prevails exclusively throughout the building, is not by any means clearly proved. It is certain, at least, that the outward aisle, upon the external wall of which is that of the building, is distinctly Saracenic in character; so also is the external panelling of the Mosque, which, though admitting it might have been afterwards cased by the Moslems, Mr. Ferguson believes will be found to be Christian. The specimen of the panelling, from Mr. Catherwood's portfolio, (p. 125,) will however clearly demonstrate that he is mistaken here. Every part of the exterior is distinctively Saracenic. It should be observed, too, that the interior arches are slightly pointed, which those of the age of Constantine are not. If the architecture is not all of one type, but of a mixed character, many other buildings of known Mohammedan origin display similar peculiarities, and *vice versa*. It has been suggested by Mr. Falkener that the edifice might have been the work of Christian builders, though employed by a Moslem master. Thus we know King Roger of Sicily employed Saracenic as well as Christian builders to erect his churches at Monreale and Palermo, which display mingled Greek and Saracenic peculiarities.

It should be observed that Mr. Ferguson is no less positive that the Mosque El Aksa is of Saracenic architecture, and not, therefore, which is generally supposed, the Church of St. Mary, built by the Emperor Justinian. Here, again, he appeals to a single view of the interior furnished by Mr. Arundale, and certainly, so far as that goes, with every appearance of reason. The general type of this building is certainly in the main Saracenic, nor can we doubt that it is the Mosque built by Abd-el-Melek-Ibn Irwan, though it has undergone some subsequent transformations and additions. But those who have gone over it affirm that the architecture is mixed, and that there are Roman as well as Saracenic pillars and capitals. It is, then, impossible that it may have been built up again, over the site, and with the materials of Justinian's Church? This is, of course, a mere suggestion, since the last-named building may really have stood where Mr. Ferguson supposes it did, a little to the eastward of the Mosque, and, like so many other churches in Jerusalem, have been entirely destroyed.

But admitting the El Aksa to be the Mosque built by Abd-el-Melek, it by no means disproves that the Dome of the Rock was also a Moslem erection; since the historical testimony quoted by Mr. Falkener is clear and explicit on this point. " According to the Muthir Alfaram, Abdul Malik-ibn-Marwan built Al Sakrah and the Temple of the Baitu-el-Mukaddas. He spent upon this building the produce of a seven years' tax upon Egypt. Again, it is said by Sabat Ibn-Jugi, in his book on the 'Changes of Dynasties,' that Abdul-Malik began the building in the year 69 Heg., and finished it in the year 72. Also, it is said, that his son, Said-ibn-Abdul-Malik-Marwan, built the chapel of the Baitu-el-Mukaddas, and its outward covering. Again, we learn from Taher-ibn-Riga, and Yazid-ibn-Salam, that Abdul-Malik wished to build a chapel upon the Sakhara of the Holy City, to be a free and lasting chapel to Mussulmen. . . . Then the Khalif assembled the best artificers of his workmen, and commanded thèm to labour diligently at the work of the chapel, *and made a vaulted crypt in it before he built the chapel.* Then laid he the foundation in the middle of the Mosque, and commanded that the Treasury (or the Dome of the Chain) should be built upon the *east side* of the Sakhara." Now the "Dome of the Chain" is, in fact, precisely east of the Mosque of Omar. Further on, the Mosque of "El Aksa," and the Chapel of the "Sakhara," are spoken of as two *distinct edifices*, as they are also by Mejir-ed-Din.

This Chapel of the Sakhara Mr. Ferguson supposes to have been merely a part of the great Mosque of El Aksa; but there is nothing to be found in it at all answering to the description given of that remarkable rock; neither is there any mention of one in the account quoted by Mr. Ferguson (Mejir). And is it probable that, if it had once existed there, the Moslems—who, with a short interval, have ever since had possession of the area —could have forgotten the original locality of this sacred rock, and transferred its situation to the present Mosque of Omar?

Mr. Ferguson further supposes the Golden Gate to be the entrance to Constantine's Basilica. This building, however, we are told, opened upon the *market-place*, which it is needless to observe could never have been near the Golden Gate. But one simple fact, sufficient of itself to overthrow the hypothesis, is this,—the caverned room in the rock of the Sakhara is *not a tomb*, neither does it in any wise resemble one. It has no couch for the reception of a body, like the sepulchres about the city. It is evidently something quite peculiar and exceptional, whatever might have been its original purpose. In the centre is the "Bir Arruah," or Well of Souls,—a deep hollow, with some mysterious subterranean communication. To suppose that such a place either was a tomb, or could ever have been regarded as such, is impossible, even if the description given by Eusebius and others of the Holy Sepulchre did not distinctly speak of a receptacle for the body found within it.

Mr. Ferguson supposes that when the Christians were expelled by the Moslems from what he believes to have been their original Church of the Sepulchre, they chose to erect a spurious one upon the present site, rather than disappoint the credulous pilgrims, or imperil the loss of their own influence. Admitting such fraud on the part of the priests and such gullibility on the part of the pilgrims were not impossible in that age, the evidence of it does not seem to be very clearly made out. Mr. Ferguson endeavours to prove a discrepancy in the accounts given of the Church of the Sepulchre by the early pilgrims, indicating that some were describing the inside of the Mosque of Omar, the original Church, and others that of the spurious one erected in imitation of it. He first appeals to Adamnanus, and to a rough plan of the Church of the Sepulchre drawn by him from memory, which, however, suits the present Church better than the Mosque, being in the first place *round*, while the second is *octangular;* so that we can see no ground for the gratuitous supposition of Mr. Ferguson, that it was from this very plan the fraudulent monks reconstructed their spurious sepulchre. Adamnanus, indeed, mentions a cave large enough to hold nine persons; but the cave itself may have been destroyed during the many changes that have happened to the Church. And this, by the way, seems almost a conclusive argument against Mr. Ferguson, that the churches of Jerusalem have so often been wholly or partially destroyed and rebuilt, whereas his ideal Church of the Sepulchre appears never to have sustained any injury during so many destructive revolutions.

As new speculation on these subjects is always interesting to many, I need offer no apology for introducing the following paper by the same erudite author to whom I have been already indebted:—

ON THE TEMPLE OF JERUSALEM, BY SAMUEL SHARPE.

"The Temple was not a covered building, as the English word might lead us to suppose. The Hebrew and Greek words mean a Holy Place, which included several courts, in one of which stood the covered building, or House of the Lord. The Temple, that is, the walls to the courts and the House, was built by Solomon about the year B.C. 1010. After its first destruction by the Babylonians in the year B.C. 588, it was rebuilt by Zerubbabel and Ezra, about B.C. 535, with little or no change in its courts. After its second destruction it was rebuilt by Herod the Great, in B.C. 14, with more magnificence than before. Herod's Temple was destroyed by the Romans under Titus; and two Turkish Mosques now stand within its holy area. But the shape of this remarkable plot of ground remains unchanged; even the foundations of the fortifications are as of old; and by the help of these and of the notices in Josephus and the Bible, we may attempt to restore the ground-plan.

We must begin with the plan and measurement of the Hill of Moriah as it now is, as we find them given in Mr. Bartlett's "Walks about Jerusalem," from Mr. Catherwood's survey.

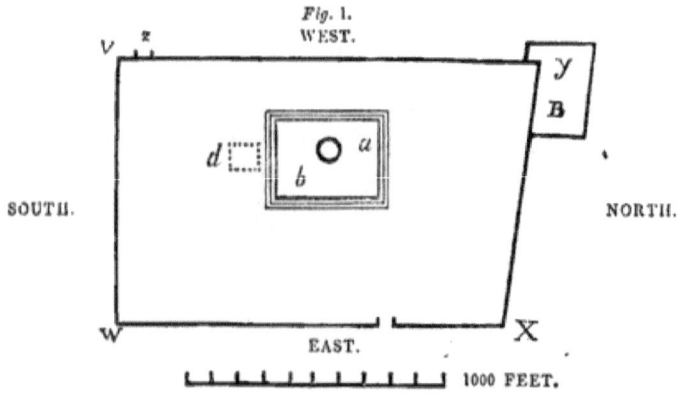

Fig. 1.

VW is the south wall, 940 feet long, with the marks of a gate now closed.

W X. The east wall, 1,520 feet long, with a gate, through which a path leads, across the valley, to the Mount of Olives. The south-east corner has been built up from the valley to make the top of the hill level.

X y. The north wall, 1,020 feet long. Beyond this is part of the city.

y V. The west wall, 1,617 feet long. A narrow valley divides this from the city.

b. A plot of ground, or rock, 15 feet high, 550 feet long, and 450 feet wide, near the middle of the hill. It is a paved platform mounted by flights of steps. On this stands the Turkish Mosque of Omar.

a. A round and flat piece of the rock, 5 feet high, and 60 feet across; now within the Mosque.

d. A plot of ground marked out as a garden. It is about 90 feet by 50.

z. Ruins of an ancient bridge across the valley from the Temple to the city.

B. The governor's house, built on ancient foundations.

The first notice that we meet with in history respecting this plot of ground is even earlier than Solomon. Part of it was the threshing-floor of Araunah, which David bought of him, and then made use of as an altar for burnt offerings to the Lord. See 2 Samuel, chapter xxiv.

a was the threshing-floor, the round piece of rocky ground, at the very top of the hill, most suitable for David's altar, as being most easily to be seen by the surrounding multitude.

When Solomon built the House of the Lord, he so placed it that this holy altar stood in the middle of a court in front of it. (1 Kings viii. 64.) He probably copied the plan of some of the Egyptian temples, the simplest of which consisted of a covered building with a court in front surrounded by a wall, or colonnade. Such are the plans of the temples of Upper Egypt. In the Temple of Bubastis, in Lower Egypt, there was a wall

THE TEMPLE.

surrounding the whole, so that the building stood not at one end of a court, as in the Theban temples, but in the middle of it.

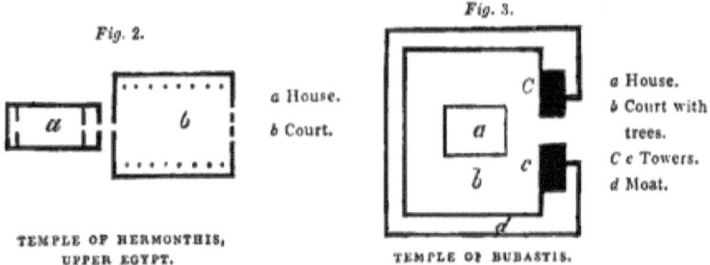

Fig. 2.
TEMPLE OF HERMONTHIS, UPPER EGYPT.
a House.
b Court.

Fig. 3.
TEMPLE OF BUBASTIS.
a House.
b Court with trees.
C c Towers.
d Moat.

Solomon's Temple, we shall see, in some respects resembled both of these. There was a court in front of the House, and a yet larger court which enclosed the House with the inner court.

We may naturally suppose that David's altar was enclosed within a fenced court, to be used by the attending priests, and the shape of the ground leads us to conjecture its size. It was, probably, the plot marked *b* in Mr. Catherwood's plan, Fig. 1. The court surrounding David's altar would of course be the court in front of the House of the Lord, when Solomon raised his building; and we shall hereafter see reasons for thinking that the House stood on the south side of the court. We thus proceed to compare our plan with the notices left to us from the history of Solomon's reign, and we make the following additions to it:—

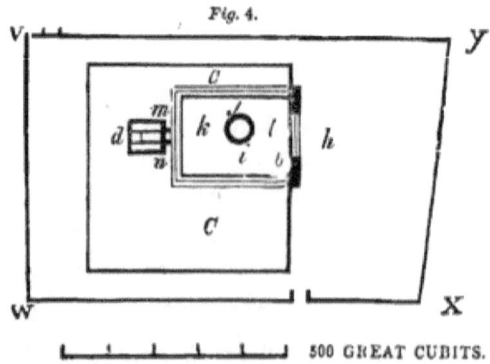

Fig. 4.
500 GREAT CUBITS.

b is the Inner Court, which was walled with three rows of hewed stone and a row of cedar posts. (1 Kings vi. 36.) This was also called the Court of the Priests. (2 Chron. iv. 9.)

d is the House of the Lord, 60 cubits long by 20 wide; or 90 feet by 30. (1 Kings vi. 2.) In front of it, towards the north, is the Porch of the House, 20 cubits wide, or as wide as the House, and 10 deep (1 Kings vi. 3); and behind is the Oracle, or place of the ark. This was 20 cubits by 20. (1 Kings vi. 19, 20.) It held the cherubim and the two tables of the law. (1 Kings viii. 6, 9.) In the Epistle to the Hebrews, it is called the Holy of Holies, (ix. 3.) On the side of the House are a number of small chambers round about the wall of the House. (1 Kings vi. 5.) These did not open into the House.

h. The Porch of the Temple, with two square pillars, each standing on a base of 50 cubits by 30. (1 Kings vii. 6.) The right-hand pillar was named Jachin, and the left pillar Boaz. (1 Kings vii. 21.) These two pillars may be explained by the pillars in front of an Egyptian temple, as in Fig. 5.

Fig. 5.

KARNAK.

m n. The places of the two pillars which stood before the House, which were not the same as the two pillars, Jachin and Boaz.

i. The place where the Levites stood, on the east side of the altar, when Solomon's new Temple was dedicated. (2 Chron. v. 12.)

j. The place where Solomon may have kneeled on his raised platform, on the same occasion. It was probably opposite to the place of the priests. (2 Chron. vi. 12, 13.) At this spot, in later days, stood the treasure-chest, for the receipt of money for the repair and maintenance of the Temple. (2 Kings xii. 9.)

k. The place where Zachariah the son of Barachiah was slain, between the altar and the House. (Matt. xxiii. 35.)

l. The place where the priests stood, when they lamented and wept, between the porch and the altar. (Joel ii. 17.) Here also, on the north side of the altar, King Ahaz placed the smaller brazen altar, when he removed it from its former place, between the altar and the House. (2 Kings xvi. 14.)

C C. The outer court, in which stood the assembled people. Its size and shape would be very much determined by the shape of the hill-top. Like the inner court, it was walled with three rows of hewed stones and a row of cedar posts. (1 Kings vii. 12.) Josephus says that this court was square, and that it measured a stadium, or about 610 feet, each way. (Antiq. XV. xi. 3.) In the above plan, for reasons afterwards to be explained, it is drawn rather larger, which seems allowable, as Josephus does not speak with exactness.

We now come to Ezekiel, who describes (chap. xl.—xlii.) a temple in a vision, by which he means to prophesy that the Temple of Jerusalem, which had been destroyed by the Babylonians, is to be rebuilt. He gives its measurements rather minutely. He makes use of the great cubit, which is a cubit and a hand-breadth in length, or, according to the Egyptian measure, $20\frac{1}{2}$ inches. He also uses the reed of six great cubits, or 10 feet 3 inches. But he was writing in banishment at a distance; and though his description may agree in its main features with the Temple which had lately been destroyed, yet we can have no certainty that he meant the measurements to be exact, even if he were acquainted with them.

Ezekiel distinguishes between the porch of the House (xl. 48) and the porch of the gate (xl. 39). This justifies our placing Solomon's porch at one end of the court, while the house is at the other.

He tells us that the altar was in front of the House (xl. 47). He says that the tables on which the people laid their offerings were in the porch of the gate, and, further, that this was the north gate of the court (xl. 35—41). This determines for us that the House was at the south end of the court.

Ezekiel's measure of the House, one hundred cubits long (xli. 13), agrees with that already quoted from the book of Kings, namely, 60 the house, 20 the porch in front, and 20 the oracle behind. His measure, however, of the inner court, which held the altar, 100 cubits long and 100 cubits broad (xl. 47), that is, 220 feet each way, makes it rather less than half the natural plot of ground which we have given to this court. On the other hand, his measure of the outer court, 500 reeds long and 500 broad (xlii. 20), that is, 5,000 feet each way, is many times as large as the space allotted to it in our plan, which is about 500 great cubits, or 850 feet each way, instead of 500 reeds.

After the time of Solomon, but long before the time of Ezekiel, the Temple-hill was enclosed within strong walls, which formed part of the fortifications of the city. They were built before the siege of Jerusalem by Sennacherib, mentioned in 2 Kings xviii. The natural shape of the ground, which falls on all sides, makes it certain that the foundations of these old walls are the same as those which are now remaining, and which are marked on the plan by the lines v w x y. Beyond these lines the outer court cannot have reached; and we must either give up the opinion that Ezekiel's measures were meant for the actual Temple, or believe that he wrote 500 cubits, instead of 500 reeds, in chap. xlii. 16—20.

After the Captivity, when the Jews had leave from the King of Persia to rebuild their Temple, in the first instance Zerubbabel was not allowed to rebuild the fortification walls, and again make it into a citadel, as it had been made after the time of Solomon. (Ezra iv. v.) These walls were, however, rebuilt by Ezra. (Nehem. ii. 17; iv. 6; xi. 16.) Ezra also made a change in the use of the building, which was called for by the religious jealousy which had grown up against the strangers in the city. He forbade the Gentiles to enter the outer court of the Temple with the Jews. They were required to stand in the space in front of the Temple, which was thus named the Court of the Gentiles. (Nehem. ix. 1, 2.) The steps to the house were now the place on which the priests stood to read the Law (Nehem. ix. 4), not as in the time of Joel, when they stood between the porch and the altar. That place was no longer the most convenient for their Jewish hearers.

After its second destruction, the Temple was built a third time by Herod. The House of the Lord was made rather larger than before. The walls of the fortifications, and of the courts, were built on the old foundations; but the whole was far more magnificent, with new cloisters and columns. Josephus describes it carefully; and with his description we must compare the notices about it in the New Testament.

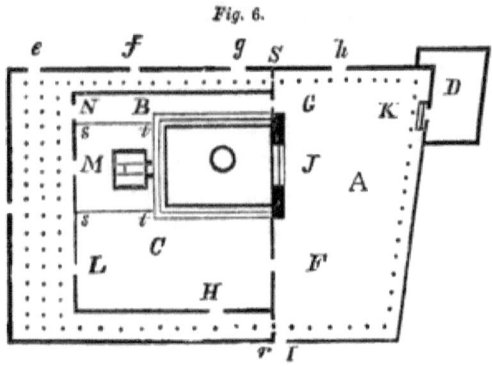

Fig. 6.

A. The Court of the Gentiles, out of which Jesus drove the money-changers. (Matt. xxi. 12.) The Pharisees, in contempt of the Gentiles, had allowed this court to be made common. Here the Saviour taught daily (xxvi. 55), and, as he was a Galilean, was probably never allowed to enter further. The Galilean apostles, when in Jerusalem, lived in fear of the Jews, or natives of Judea. (See John xx. 19.)

q r. The middle wall of the partition, beyond which Jews only might pass. (Antiq. XV. xi. 5.) Paul, speaking figuratively, said that Jesus had removed this wall. (Ephes. ii. 14.) This was built in a more massive way than the other three sides of the Temple proper, so that with the fortified walls around the hill, it formed a fortress by itself, independent of the court of the Gentiles.

Thus in the Gospels, and by the enlightened Paul, the court of the Gentiles is called a part of the Temple. But it was not so before the time of Nehemiah, nor in the Acts of the Apostles; when Paul is accused of taking Greeks into the Temple, it meant that he took them beyond the middle wall. (Acts xxi. 28.) So also the soldiers of Titus are said to fight between the Castle and the Temple. Josephus was too strict a Jew to call the court of the Gentiles part of the holy place. (Wars, VI. ii. 6.) In the book of Revelation, the doubt in the meaning of the word is acknowledged; but the writer does not wish the wall of partition to be removed. He says, " Rise, and measure the Temple of God, and the altar, and them that worship therein. But the court without the Temple leave out, and measure it not; for it is given to the Gentiles." (Chap. xi. 1.)

$B\ C$. The courts into which Jews might enter. Women as well as men might enter the court C. (Josephus, Antiq. XV. xi. 5.)

$F\ G\ J$. The three gates on the north side. (*Ibid.*)

$L\ M\ N$. The three gates on the south side. (*Ibid.*)

H. The large gate through which men and women might both enter. It faced the east. (*Ibid.*) This may have been the Beautiful Gate, at which the beggar sat to ask alms. (Acts iii. 2.) He probably sat where women passed as well as men.

D. The castle built by the Maccabees. (Antiq. XV. xi. 4.) It was called by Herod the Castle of Antonia. On its foundations the governor's house now stands.

K. The castle steps, where Paul stood to speak to the people. (Acts xxi. 40.) So he was carried by the soldiers across the court of the Gentiles, from F or G, the gate through which he was accused of taking Greeks.

I. The gate from the Mount of Olives, through which Jesus

entered the Temple every morning during the last Passover. (Luke xxi. 37.) He there taught daily in the court of the Gentiles.

J. Solomon's porch, where the apostles taught the people. (Acts v. 12.) This is particularly described in Ezekiel (chap. xl. 39—43), with the hooks and tables for the meat-offerings. It was then called the Porch of the Gate.

e. The gate which led from the king's palace, by a bridge over the valley, to the Temple, and through the royal cloisters. (Antiq. XV. xi. 5.)

f g h may be the three other gates on that side.

Herod's cloisters ran all round the walls with a single row of columns; they were 30 feet wide. At the south end they were called the royal cloisters, and were formed of three rows of columns.

If we now review the reasons for giving its size and shape to the Temple proper, in Fig. 6, we remark that Josephus and Ezekiel both say that it was square; that it certainly stood within the fortification walls on the Temple-hill, so that it could not be larger than 900 feet square; and when we allow for the pavement, and the cloisters between this square inclosure and the fortifications, it may even have been less; and that Josephus says it was a *stadium*, or 610 feet square. Ezekiel, on the other hand, says that it was 500 reeds, or 5,000 feet square; but if we suppose that we ought to read 500 great cubits, it was 850 feet square. In Fig. 6 it is drawn about 900 feet square.

That the court of the altar was not surrounded by the square inclosure of the Temple, but at one end, seems meant by Josephus, who describes the courts on each side of the court of the altar, but mentions no space in front of it. If it were otherwise, Gentiles could not have brought their offerings directly to the priests, as we see in Ezekiel was the case. And this arrangement leaves just the space needed for the royal cloisters on the south, and for the court of the Gentiles on the north.

There were also two other walls (perhaps *s t*), which placed the house within a court of its own, separated from the courts of the men and women. It was, perhaps, the court of the priests. Herod, not being a priest, was excluded from three places,—the court of the altar, the court of the priests, and the house of the Lord. (Antiq. XV. xi. 6.)"

In taking leave of the Mosque of Omar we may observe that, besides being an edifice for religious worship, its large square, on two sides, is lined with houses of hospitality, originally intended for residence of learned men and servants of the whole institution, who were to be maintained from the ample endowments of land and houses in various parts, not only of this country, but of other Moslem lands also.

The administration is now greatly altered from the original intention of the endowments. The property is united in one with that of the Haram of Hebron.

The income is at present about 3,500*l.* annually, but with good management it might be easily raised to 5,000*l.*: not more, however, than 100*l.* is spent annually upon the institution; the rest is transmitted to Constantinople, a practice that was commenced about fifty years since.

No learned Shaikhs now receive salaries or support of any kind from the endowment. The families entitled from ancient times to receive pensions for hereditary offices, have had those allowances greatly curtailed. The servants are paid at the lowest possible rate, or in some cases only fed from the Tekeeyeh; and the building is falling to decay.

Besides this, and the "Tekeeyeh" and "Neby Daood," elsewhere alluded to, there is the *Dair el Hinood*, situated in the highest part of the Bab Hotta quarter. This is a residence or hospice for Moslem pilgrims from India. Generally the inmates are but few, and not of long continuance here. The establishment possesses some land, (*i.e.* foundations of old houses,) and two scarcely tenantable houses, as property within the walls of the city. And here also is the *Yuzbekeeyeh*, with a pleasant garden, adjoining the Pasha's seraglio. The inmates are pilgrims from Tartary, Bokhara, &c.; these seldom exceed half-a-dozen in number, and the place has a small property of houses in the town for its maintenance.

Both the Tartar and Indian pilgrims within the city are engaged in various occupations for earning a livelihood; some sell beads and trinkets of agate, cornelian, &c., in the bazaars. Besides the more prominent institutions, every Mosque in the city has some Wak'f, or landed property, for its support; but this is much neglected or pilfered. Thus it would appear that the charitable and religious foundations of the Turks in Jerusalem are falling to decay, while those of the various sects of Christians are rising into greater importance.

CHAPTER VI.

Matters Miscellaneous.

TOPOGRAPHY OF ANCIENT CITY—WALK ROUND THE WALLS—JEREMIAH'S CAVE
—DAMASCUS GATE—ANCIENT CHAMBERS—NORTH-WEST CORNER—EXCURSION TO THE CONVENT OF THE CROSS—STATE OF FEELING IN JERUSALEM—
JEALOUSIES AND REPORTS—ROAD TO JAFFA BY BETHHORON AND LYDDA.

In glancing at the map of Jerusalem, and observing how strongly marked is its site by the hand of nature, and how limited, from the character of the ground, must have been its dimensions; one might suppose that there is no city of the ancient world, respecting the topography of which there was room for so little question; yet, strange to say, although this general correspondence of situation between the ancient city and the modern is evident, and admitted by everybody, there is perhaps no similar instance in which so many conflicting notions have been put forth, respecting the course of the three walls, and the position of the prominent buildings. It would seem as if this limited space were destined to be an arena for the eternal display of antiquarian ingenuity and learning,—the battle ground of views diametrically opposed to each other; and so inexhaustible appears to be the fascination of the subject, that fresh theories continue to be poured forth, each of them more absurd—or, to speak more respectfully of the learned disputants – at least more startling than that which preceded it. The lines of the three walls have been drawn in every direction that ingenuity could devise, no two of them altogether alike. The spots of the crucifixion and burial of our Lord are still maintained by many to be correctly situated in the Church of the Holy Sepulchre, and by others placed at almost every imaginable point about the neighbourhood of the city. Even the site and dimensions of the Temple itself, which one might imagine to be the easiest to settle, is matter of hardly less dispute, being placed by some on the northern, by some on the southern frontier of the great enclosure, while others still place it in the centre. Some assign to it limits almost as extensive, and others restrict it to a comparatively narrow portion. The character of the buildings within and about it are no less the subject of controversy, and one of the latest and most skilfully elaborated theories is, that the building hitherto regarded as the Mosque of Omar, is no other than the true Church of Constantine, built over the genuine sepulchre of Jesus! But it would require a volume merely to enumerate these jarring speculations, and nothing could render them even intelligible, far less interesting, but a visit to the spot itself. In such a state of incertitude, the wisest plan is, perhaps, to echo the opinion of Mejir-ed-Din, in speaking of a particular edifice, " It was *perhaps* built by the founder of that school, *but God knows best!* "

For these conflicting ideas about the topography of the Holy City, two causes, (besides the passion for theorising,) may be assigned: First, the alteration of the ground, destruction of buildings, and blending of different monuments and styles, wrought by the destructive revolutions of two thousand years; till perhaps hardly a fragment of what Jerusalem once was remains unaltered—and mountains of disfiguring rubbish have everywhere accumulated; and, Secondly, the difficulty of reconciling the descriptions of the city given us by Josephus with the nature of the ground, at least as it is at the present day. Writing from mere memory, at a distance from the spot itself, with an evident tendency to exaggerate, sometimes contradicting himself, often very loose and unscientific in his definitions, and having palpably omitted many particulars essential to a clear understanding of the subject, nothing can be more evident, than to apply his descriptions, (originally imperfect,) to a widely different state of things, with any *exact precision*, is a task almost, if not entirely, hopeless. Indeed, could the learned Jew himself come to life again, and revisit the city he has described, it is probable he would be often as much puzzled to retrace his old landmarks amidst the desolations of ages, as his commentators have been before him.

Such being the uncertainty in which the question is involved, we shall not attempt to increase it by proposing any new theories; but very briefly explain those, between which opinion is generally divided.

Almost all writers on the subject agree in regarding the present Mount Zion as identical with that of the Old Testament.

The first exception is Dr. Clarke, who places it upon the Hill of Evil Counsel, regarding the deep valley of Hinnom as the Tyropeon of Josephus, which divided the city, and of which the sides were so steep that the streets broke off abruptly on either hand. The second is Mr. Ferguson, who, strangely enough, supposes that it occupied part of the site of the Temple Mount itself. Neither of these views deserves the trouble of a serious refutation.

Assuming, then, the identity of Mount Zion, it is supposed that the old, or *First Wall*, which originally encircled the stronghold of David, must have followed nearly the present line of wall from the north-west angle of the city to the Jaffa Gate, and so passing by the castle of David, or citadel; but beyond that, it included at least the whole of the level ground on the top of Mount Zion, at present excluded from the walls. Some suppose that it ran down the steep ground, so as to enclose the Pools of Siloam and the Virgin, ascending from the latter fountain up to the southern angle of the Temple; thus enclosing a very considerable space, which, though rugged, was available for buildings. By others it is supposed to have excluded the pools, and taking nearly the same line, to have joined the Temple wall at or near the same point as at present.

On the other hand, it is believed that this wall, starting from near the present corner, bent round along the abrupt ridge of Mount Zion, just above the street of David, and thence descended to some point on the western wall of the Temple. A bridge traversed the intervening hollow, and united Zion and Moriah. As when this bridge was forced by Titus, he had still to besiege the upper city, it would appear, that there must have been also a continuation of this old wall to a junction with the other part below; as otherwise Zion would have been evidently open and undefended, yet no such wall is anywhere mentioned by Josephus.

The *Second Wall*, we are told by that writer, started off from the old one at a gate called Gennath, or the Gate of the Gardens, and took a curving direction round to the Fort Antonia, which stood at the north-west angle of the Temple area. Supposing this gate Gennath to have been at a point near the north-west extremity of the walls, opening into a tract of gardens, and including the pool, commonly called the Pool of Hezekiah, it would probably have followed, for obvious defensive reasons, the same line as the present wall, as far as the Damascus Gate. If we are to follow Josephus literally, it must thence have made a curve to the present site of the governor's house, where the Antonia is believed to have stood. It is almost incredible, however, that this should ever have been the case; not only because the space thus inclosed would be far too much to answer our ideas of the capital of Solomon and Herod, but because also it would abandon the obviously advantageous line followed by the existing wall, for one precisely the contrary. And, perhaps, we should not be very far out in supposing that the present wall runs nearly on the line of the old one, and that Bezetha was included within the city.

Those, however, who contend for the authenticity of the Holy Sepulchre, which, as we *know*, stood somewhere outside this same second wall, are of course obliged to shape its course so as to exclude the Church. In order to effect this, they place the gate Gennath further east along the old wall, and from that point run a line to the Damascus Gate, nearly along the present bazaar, which, after all, *barely* accomplishes the object of leaving the church outside. From the Damascus Gate to the Antonia they follow nearly the same line as the others; but not only is the space thus enclosed absolutely insignificant, but the line it follows is objectionable in a defensive light, being overlooked and commanded by higher ground.

Respecting the *Third Wall*, constructed by Agrippa, after our Saviour's death, to enclose the populous northern suburbs, there is little or no disagreement. It is generally believed to have followed still further the ridge north-west of the city, up to a high culminating point, where stood the Tower of Psephinus, somewhere near to a small Arab tomb. Thence it bent across to the royal sepulchres, probably the present "Tombs of the Kings," and thence along the ridge of the Valley of Jehoshaphat, till it formed a junction with the second wall.

Another point, disputed of late with some acrimony, is the true direction of the Tyropeon, or Valley of Cheesemongers, already described as separating the *upper* from the *lower* city. At the present day, there is no valley within the limits of the city answering to the description already quoted from Josephus; viz., that it was so precipitous that the streets broke off on either side. When, however, we consider that the rubbish of ages has accumulated over this surface, it is not surprising that such a valley should be filled up. Perhaps, after all, the description of Josephus was only applicable to the lowest part of the Tyropeon, (then perhaps situated within, but at present without the walls,) to the abrupt acclivities of which it perfectly corresponds.

As there are no marked natural features to identify this valley, we must look to the description given of its site by Josephus. He tells us that it separated the upper from the lower city, which latter, inferior in height, was north of Zion, and west of the Temple. Nothing at all appears to answer to these conditions but the line of street running down beneath the brow of Zion, from the supposed Tower of Hippicus to the Temple. In this case we have Zion on one side, and Acra, or the Lower City, on the other, due west of the Temple, extending over an inferior swell of ground down to the Damascus Gate, and divided from Moriah and Bezetha by the broad valley running right through the city from the Damascus Gate to Siloam.

According to the theory of Mr. Williams, this last-mentioned valley is itself the true Tyropeon, and that of Dr. Robinson purely imaginary. If this were really the case, we should be obliged, in order to meet Josephus's conditions—that the valley divided Zion and Acra—to extend the limits of the former over all that space which, in the first theory, is supposed to be Acra; and to transplant this latter to a mere corner of land on the opposite side of the valley, lying north and not west of the Temple, and east and not north of Zion.

In choosing between these two theories, it may be observed that while Dr. Robinson entirely satisfies Josephus's topographical bearings, that of Mr. Williams is as obviously opposed to them; on the other hand, there is, undoubtedly, more of the appearance of a valley in Mr. Williams's Tyropeon, than in that of Dr. Robinson; but of this we shall speak more fully in describing that locality.

St. Stephen's Gate is at the present day the only one open on the eastern side of the city. It received its name from the tradition that St. Stephen was dragged through it, (or one formerly existing on the site,) outside the walls of the city, and stoned at a short distance. It is unquestionable that the church dedicated to the protomartyr, and built by Eudoxia over the spot *miraculously* revealed to Lucian, stood on the western side of the city. After its destruction, the tradition of the martyrdom was unaccountably transferred to the present gate, indicating, as it does too plainly, the readiness with which holy places were moved about in the dark ages, often to suit the convenience or cupidity of ecclesiastics, and how little value is consequently to be attached to their local traditions. This transference has been regarded by Mr. Williams, the great advocate of ecclesiastical infallibility, as an *unfortunate* mistake; to efface the memory of which, as far as possible, he has rechristened the gate after the name of St. Mary, whose traditional tomb, itself of equal authenticity, is situated in the valley below.

Following the outside of the wall, bordered with cemeteries, and passing a small pool, we gradually ascend to the north-east angle of the city wall, which here displays no traces of a date anterior to that of the Saracens. At the angle, and for some distance along its northern face, which we now continue to trace, it is protected by a fosse; but beyond this point it is greatly strengthened by resting on a foundation of rock, which rises gradually until it becomes a precipitous cliff; and opposite to which is another rocky ridge, between which passes the roadway leading round the city. Before reaching the highest point, we pass one of the gates, now closed, called Bab-el-Zahar, or the Gate of Herod. The character of this part of the walls, which is very striking, is well displayed from a cavern in a ridge of rocks on the opposite side of the road. To our own mind, the conviction was irresistible on the spot, that this rocky ridge, affording as it does so strong a defensive position, must have been adopted by the builders of the second wall. And here, accordingly, it is laid down by Schultz in his map, with every appearance of local evidence, but certainly is little in harmony with the statement of Josephus, who describes this wall as taking a curve from Hippicus to the Antonia, unless, indeed, we give a convenient latitude to his meaning.

The wall between this point and the north-east angle of the

city has a special interest, as being doubtless that where Godfrey of Bouillon succeeded in forcing his entrance into the city, by means of towers, from which bridges were thrown upon the wall. Saladin, also, made his attack at the same point, and not impossibly Titus before both, if we, after leaving the third wall, are correct in believing that the old second wall may have originally taken this direction.

One of the most remarkable features of the environs of Jerusalem is certainly the number of natural caverns, or caves, enlarged by art, either as habitations for the living, or as the receptacles of the dead. In whatever direction the visitor may perambulate the city, he is startled with the yawning mouths of subterranean hollows unexpectedly opening beneath him, while every hill-side is perforated by rock-hewn sepulchres and grottos. Among the most striking is that traditionally called the Cave of Jeremiah. It is deeply sunk in a ridge of rock, the top of which is used as a burying ground, rising opposite to this part of the northern wall. The entrance is defended by a wall, which is usually kept locked by the keeper of the cave, who lives within. On obtaining access, the effect of the overhanging masses of rock, perforated by the profound and gloomy cavern, is strikingly impressive. Part of the space at the entrance has been converted to the purposes of a Lazaretto, by constructing several walled divisions or rooms, to which the overhanging rock itself serves as a roof. On passing these, we found the cavern supported by two immense pillars of rock, the view of which, with the sunlight faintly struggling into the mouth of the cavern, formed a picture of very striking effect. It is supposed by some, that great part of the cave has been hollowed out; but it is more probably natural, with some assistance from art. The tradition that connects it with the Prophet Jeremiah is evidently arbitrary and baseless, as also that which gives his name to a small pool on the opposite side of the road. In the rock near it are two other double caverns, bearing still greater marks of laborious excavation and ornament. Caverns of a similar kind, but subterranean, are to be found in the side of the Valley of Jehoshaphat, not far from the north-east angle of the city.

On the rocky hill over the cave is a Mahommedan burial-ground, called the Turbet-ez-Zahara.

Descending from Jeremiah's Cave, we strike into the broad and shallow valley which intersects the city, to Siloam, in the hollow of which stands the Babel Amud, or Gate of Damascus, the only one open on the north-west face of the city. This is undeniably the handsomest of all the gates of Jerusalem; and, with its flanking towers, adorned with bold projections and crenulated battlements, presents a striking specimen of Arabian architecture.

The arch of this gate is considered by Mr. Catherwood as one of those specimens conclusively proving that the pointed arch had its origin in Syria. He considers the earliest pointed arches to be found at Jerusalem, whence they were carried by the

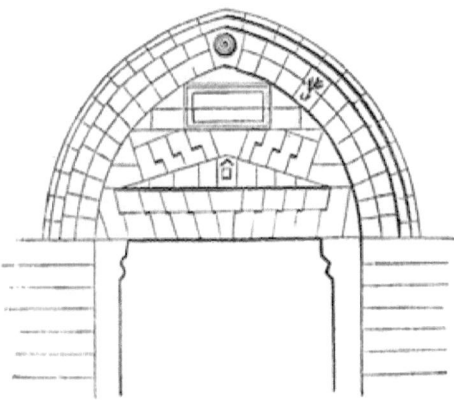

Crusaders to different parts of Christendom. The so-called Gothic architecture he regards as undoubtedly derived from this source. The pointed arch he supposes to have preceded the horseshoe modification of it adopted by the Saracens. The peculiar masonry above the door and within the arch resembles

that on the monument of Theodoric, at Ravenna, who died in the year 526.

At the base of the towers, near the gateway, (and shown in the drawing,) may be seen two or three of those massive stones, which bear the undoubted stamp of the Jewish times, and were most probably brought from a ruined chamber not far off, which will be noticed elsewhere, though I must confess myself unable, (as was also my companion,) to discover any other of these vestiges along the face of the north-western wall, as some other travellers profess to have done before us.

Besides the traces of large stones in the Damascus Gate, there is a remarkable specimen of them just within, in some ancient chambers discovered by Dr. Robinson, and the description of which it is proper to give in his own words. "Every traveller," he remarks, "has probably observed the large ancient hewn stones which lie just in the inside of that gate towards the east. In looking at them one day, and passing round them, we were surprised to find there a square dark room adjacent to the wall, the sides of which are entirely composed of stone having precisely the character of those still seen at the corners of the Temple area,—large, bevelled, with the whole surface hewn smooth, and thus exhibiting an earlier and more careful style of architecture than those remaining in the tower of Hippicus. Connected with this room, on the west side, is a winding staircase leading to the top of the wall, the sides of which are of the same character. Following out this discovery, we found upon the western side of the gate, though further from it, another room of precisely the same kind, corresponding in all respects to that upon the eastern side, except that it had been much more injured in building the present wall, and is in part broke away. Of the stones, one measured $7\frac{1}{2}$ feet long by $3\frac{1}{2}$ feet high, and another $6\frac{1}{2}$ feet long by a like height. Some of them are much disintegrated and decayed, but they all seem to be lying in their original places, as if they had never been disturbed nor moved from the spot where they were first fitted to each other. The only satisfactory conjecture which I can form respecting these structures is, that they were ancient towers of a date anterior to the time of Herod, and probably the guard-houses of an ancient gate upon this spot. This gate could have belonged only to the second wall."

In a note, the learned professor admits that it is possible, though not probable, that they might have been rebuilt by Adrian, from old materials. The annexed view will enable the reader to form his own conclusion on this point. The stones at all events are the same as those of the Temple enclosure; and if not in their original position, testify, at the least, to the existence of massive edifices near the spot, of which they are the remains; most probably belonging, as Dr. Robinson supposes, to the second wall.

Leaving the Damascus Gate, the road round the walls ascends the opposite side of the hollow until it gains their north-west angle, which rests upon the highest ground in the city; being a bold ridge which rises between the hollow just mentioned, and the deeper one of the Valley of Hinnom, and forming so obviously the strongest defensive position on this side of the city.

The towers at this angle, which show no traces of Jewish masonry, rest, as may easily be seen, upon a foundation of rock, and are besides strengthened with a sort of natural fosse. Opposite to them rises a large Terebinth-tree, conspicuous in every view of the city. Just within this point are found the ruins of the "Giant's Castle," or "Tancred's Tower," as it is also called; from the fact that the forces of that chieftain were arranged without it, at the siege of Jerusalem under Godfrey of Bouillon.

Here we diverged from the north-west wall, (which presents nothing remarkable as far as the Jaffa Gate, and runs probably nearly if not quite on the same line as the old one,) and directed our steps along the ridge to the north-west, with a view to trace the line of the third, or Agrippa's wall, round to its junction

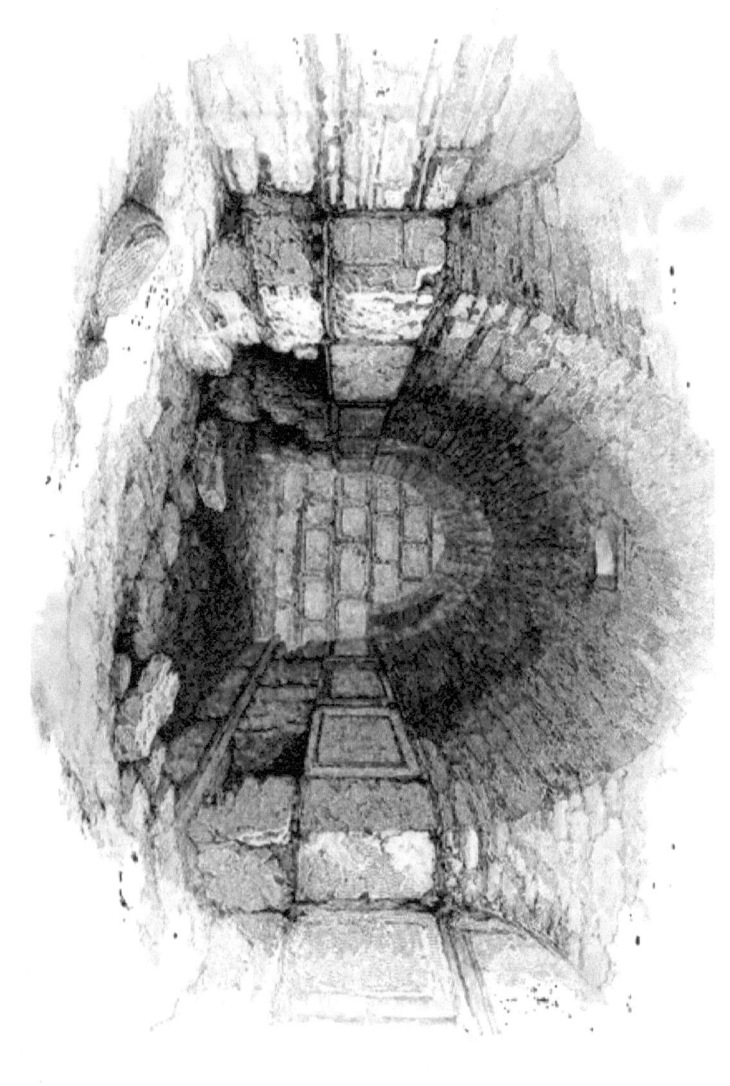

WALL OF AGRIPPA.

with the north-east wall, at the point already mentioned. The vestiges of buildings, and occasional appearances as though the rock had been scraped for foundations, indicated beyond all doubt the general direction of this outer bulwark, as far as an elevated point, where probably stood the tower of Psephinus, commanding, as Josephus informs us, a view from the sea to the Arabian mountains. From hence we beat round, across fields of barley sprinkled with clumps of olive-trees, coming upon tanks, and other traces of ground formerly occupied by buildings, until we reached the Tombs of the Kings; near, or indeed past which (if we are correct in regarding them as the royal sepulchres), Josephus informs us that the wall continued its course. Hence there could be no doubt that it would be drawn along the precipitous brink of the upper Valley of Jehoshaphat, and continue to follow it to the north-east corner of the city.

One thing that cannot fail to strike any one who looks at the map of Jerusalem, is the immense additional space this third wall of Agrippa appears to have enclosed, in proportion to the limits of the city walls, in the palmy days of Herod, a space, in fact, nearly equal to the whole of the modern city; and, (if we are to accept the views generally entertained as to the limited extent of the second wall,) no less of the ancient Jerusalem also. It is true, that the suburbs had become very extensive; but yet, so excessive a disproportion seems hardly credible, when we consider that, in the days of Herod, the city was strong and extensive, and had attained the very climax of splendour and populousness. I cannot but suppose, that the north-west corner of the city, with the towers of Hippicus, Phasalus and Mariamne, must then have extended at least as far as at present; and that the second wall must have taken a wider sweep than is generally supposed, following nearly the same line as that of the modern city. And this opinion is fortified by the fact, that it is actually the best defensive line that could be adopted, without enclosing a very much greater space. Besides that, in general, the builders of a new wall would naturally take advantage of the foundations of an old one.

In perambulating the environs of the city in this direction, especially above the Valley of Hinnom, I was agreeably struck with the great increase of planting upon the hill-sides, which at the period of my first visit were totally uncultivated. Notwithstanding the unpromising ruggedness of the surface, the vine and olive have been taught to take root in the scanty but prolific soil, restoring to the environs, in some measure at least, the cultivated beauty which they no doubt exhibited in the flourishing days of Jerusalem; and showing what may be realized whenever the pursuits of peaceful industry shall receive a greater impulse and a surer protection. These improvements are principally the work of the Greeks, who have not only planted pretty extensively, but have made large purchases of land in the neighbourhood of the city, to a degree that is not generally suspected. All this it is believed has been done with Russian gold, and for the spread of Russian influence.

One of the pleasant spots within a short distance of Jerusalem is the Convent of the Cross. It is seen on the right in approaching the city by the Jaffa road, prettily retired in a valley. Riding out one afternoon in company with a friend, in about twenty minutes we reached the sheltered hollow in which it is situated. Like all the convents in Palestine so exposed to the Moslem invasion, its walls are of immense solidity, having few openings by which an entrance could be effected. Notwithstanding this, the Arabs, a few years since, contrived to make an entrance and murder the superior. The best view is from a rising ground, whence it appears to great advantage, half-buried in olive groves, with a back-ground of rocky hills.

On obtaining the key, we passed through an outer court, and reached the church, with the size and ornament of which we were really surprised. The mosaic pavement was superior to any

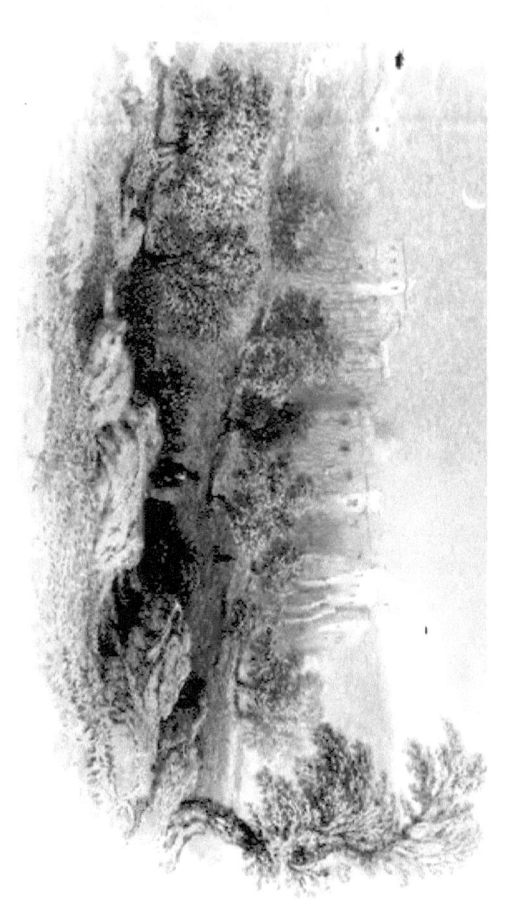

in Jerusalem. We were now conducted to the spot from which the convent derived its name; for it would have been strange, indeed, if an age which witnessed the discovery, or, as it is otherwise called, the *invention* of the Holy Cross, should have failed to discover also the precise spot where grew the tree of which it was made; which accordingly is pointed out in a vault behind the altar.

Maundrell speaks of this spot somewhat irreverently, parodying a well-known rhyme. " The convent," he says, " is neat in its structure, and in its situation delightful; but that which most deserves to be noted in it, is the reason of its name and foundation. It is because there is the earth that nourished the root, that bore the tree, that yielded the timber, that made the cross. Under the high altar you are shown a hole in the ground where the stump of the tree stood; and it meets with not a few visitants, so much more very stocks than itself as to fall down and worship it."

This convent, of late tenanted only by two or three monks, is at present (1853) used for more beneficial purposes, being adopted as the clerical seminary and day-school of the Greek Christians. This institution was founded about four years ago, but only came into fair operation last year. The day-school has ninety pupils, under four masters. The highest range of Greek classics is here studied, together with German, French, geography, arithmetic, &c. Costly roads leading to it, besides plantations, are being made, under the especial patronage of Russia.

The Convent of the Cross is mentioned by Sæwulf, who says that it had been ravaged by the Pagans, but that the destruction fell chiefly on the conventual buildings; the church, more fortunate than many others, having been in great measure spared. It is the only remaining seat of the Georgians, an ancient orthodox church, which formerly possessed an influence at Jerusalem, at present almost entirely lost. The site of the convent was granted to them by Constantine; and it was erected by their king, Tatian, in the fifth century.

The impression produced upon me by Jerusalem was—even more than at first—that of peculiar sadness and oppressive gloom. This might partly be owing to the bareness of the surrounding country, and the total absence of beauty, but principally to something in the very physiognomy of the place itself; its gloomy sunken glens, its narrow fetid streets, and its ever recurring traces of revolution and conflict. Of all cities in the world, it has the distinction of being the battle-ground for religious creeds—the field where the fanaticism of the Jew, the Christian, and the Turk has met, and alternately triumphed. No spot of its size on earth has been so soaked with blood; no city has been the theatre of so many awful tragedies. The scars of all this warfare, and the stains of all this bloodshed, will not wear out, but seem indelibly impressed upon the place. The very air seems sadder than elsewhere, and the physiognomy of the people has on it a kindred gloom. The poor Jew seems to wander about the place with that face of unrest, the index to the "astonishment of heart" to which he is judicially sentenced. Sullen bigotry is in the face of the monks, latent fanaticism in the eye of the Moslems, poverty in the look of all the people. No traces of lightness of spirit, of joyousness of heart, are anywhere discernible; nothing but a mournful stillness, which gradually falls like a cloud over the spirit of the traveller, and reminds him he is in a city over which the curse still seems to hang.

The time of my departure from Jerusalem now drew near The state of the country was becoming very unsettled, and the bazaars were filled with all sorts of idle and extravagant reports. The innkeepers and dealers in pious ware, who depend so much on pilgrims and travellers, were in a state of consternation, lest with the breaking out of war the usual influx of visitors should be partly, if not entirely, stopped. Some who had usually encamped out of the city at this season, preferred to remain within the walls.

As an instance of the distorted rumours floating about during our stay at Jerusalem, we may cite the following, which was supposed to have originated, as much spurious information is said to do, at the Austrian consulate: "There would be no war, since it was agreed, *with the consent of England and France*, that Russia should take possession of the Danubian Principalities." Although the falsity of this must have been evident to any one at all acquainted with the subject, it was for some days currently believed by most people in the city. One day, we were frightened from our propriety by the news that the Turks had risen, and were murdering the Christians at Jaffa; nor was it till we arrived there, that this was proved to be a false alarm. Nothing of the sort had happened, if we except one or two stray murders outside the town, of which, in this country, little or no account is made. Yet this false report so terrified the wife of a French doctor living at Jaffa, that, hearing a noise, and fancying the massacre was just beginning, she leaped out of the window and broke a limb, and was still lying in a very dangerous state.

It was generally admitted that the Franks and Jews in Jerusalem, *if they held together*, were quite able to keep the Turkish population in check, should fanaticism drive them to insurrection. The convents are so many fortresses; and it was said that the monks were well supplied with arms. The citadel, besides, was too strong to be taken without artillery; and the Fellaheen, when they took the city in Ibrahim Pacha's time, were unable to get possession of this stronghold. I was besides informed, upon good authority, that such was the influence of the English consul, that he had received assurances from many of the neighbouring sheiks that they would instantly answer to his call, in case of any rising in the country. Still it was to be feared, at the least, that, (as at all periods of disturbance under a weak government,) local quarrels would arise, old feuds be revived, robbers appear upon the roads, and general disorder and insecurity prevail, even if the members of the English consulate and mission were enabled to remain at Jerusalem.

There are two roads leading from Jaffa to Jerusalem: the shorter, but more rugged, through Ramleh and Kuryet-el-Enab; the other, about two hours longer, but much easier, is by way of Beit-ur (Bethhoron), and Ludd (Lydda). Having twice taken the former, we now preferred to take the latter, on returning to join the steamer at Jaffa.

Attended only by the Makharah, and a respectable Turk, whose company was considered desirable in the event of interruption on the way, I left Jerusalem about nine in the morning. Our road, or rather track, lay across the open ground west of the city; and for a considerable distance beyond what are usually considered its utmost limits in this direction, we continued to meet with cisterns, tombs cut in the rock, and other suburban traces. Before leaving the high ground we obtained a parting view of the domes and towers of the Holy City; and then descended into a deep valley, presenting the same prevalence of rock, interspersed here and there with patches of arable land and olive groves. After passing the village of Beit Hanina, we saw above us, on our left, the lofty summit of Neby Samwit—the ancient Mizpah, as Robinson supposes. It is surmounted by a mosque, containing the traditional tomb of the prophet Samuel. Shortly afterward, we approached another village perched on a rocky hill, being El Jib, or the Gibeon of the Old Testament. The road, however, passes along its base; and we made here a short halt under an olive-tree, by the side of an ancient fountain.

Resuming our journey, we skirted an open fertile plain; beyond which, the view of these ancient biblical localities was very striking. Shortly after, we reached the culminating point of the high ground between Jerusalem and the plains; and obtained a distant view over the intervening hills to the sea coast. The road, though rocky and difficult, as are those of Palestine in general, was far easier than that by Jaffa; avoiding the precipitous ascents and descents of the latter, and being carried gradually along the ridges of the hills. From the earliest times down to the present day, it has accordingly been the track for heavily laden caravans, and for the march of troops. It was by this road that St. Paul was sent by night from Jerusalem to Cæsarea, escorted by a body of soldiers.

Soon after reaching the crest of the hill, we saw before us, a mile or two beyond, the village of Beit-'ur-el-Fôka, or Upper Bethhoron, standing out on a bold prominence against the distant horizon. On the left of the ridge we were following, was a deep valley, the Wady Suleiman, down which passes a branch of the road which rejoins the other, not far from Lydda. It was a question, whether it was in this pass, or the one we were taking, that the terrible rout of Cesbues, the Roman proconsul, by the Jews, took place.

The approach to Upper Bethhoron is one of the most striking scenes in Palestine. The village, crowned with a tower, occupies the top of the hill, from which the ground descends abruptly on every side. Beyond, the hill-country of Judea sinks gradually into the plains of the sea-coast, in a succession of wavy slopes and ridges, which even now look beautiful; and in those days, when the cultivation of the country was well attended to, must have vied with the richest of similar landscapes.

Although the village of Upper Bethhoron displays no monuments, the traces of old stones built into its humble cottages indicate that it is an ancient site. The slopes of the hill on which it stands are clothed with olive and fig-trees. At an ancient reservoir, by the wayside, we watered our horses; and then began the descent of the pass, which still keeps a sloping direction down the ridge, above deep valleys on either side. Beit-'ur-et-Tahta, Bethhoron the Lower, now appeared on the other side of a hollow, on another space of the same ridge. Between these villages lay the famous pass of Bethhoron, which affords the easiest access from the hill region of Jerusalem to the plains along the shore, except the Wady Suleiman, which runs a short distance to the south.

We paused a few moments at Bethhoron the Lower, which is also a small village; and, still descending, followed the course of a valley winding out gradually to the level of the plain. The sun set as we ascended a ridge, and passed over what was evidently an ancient site; now partly occupied with a modern village which commands a striking view of the walls. The tower of Kanila, and the tall minaret of Ludd, were dimly discernible across the plain, before we were enveloped in the shades of twilight; and in about ten hours' ride from Jerusalem, we descended from horseback at the fountain outside the town of Ludd.

Tired out by a long ride under a burning sun, we found great difficulty in obtaining any sort of lodging. Besides, there happened to be a Turkish festival; the bazaars were crowded with people; and the heat from the numerous lamps, added to the confined atmosphere of these alleys on a close night in summer, would have rendered it impossible to sleep. I sighed as I thought of the comfortable convent at Ramleh; and after much research bestowed myself upon the flat roof of the ruined Seraiyah; which, if it presented no other advantages, had at least that of being cool and pleasant, and commanding a splendid view of the stars. Wrapped up in a cloak, I here lay down until the early dawn should enable us to pursue our journey.

Lydda is celebrated in New Testament history as the place where St. Peter healed Eneas; it was called Diospolis under the Romans, and erected into a Christian bishopric; but it was chiefly famous in connexion with St. George, the patron saint of England. He is said to have been born at Lydda; and after his martyrdom at Nicomedia, in the persecution of Diocletian, his remains were brought here for sepulture. A splendid tomb arose over his ashes, and a church was erected in his honour, the ruins of which are still to be seen in the town.

We were prevented from visiting these interesting relics by the necessity of reaching Jaffa very early in the morning. While the stars were yet shining, we mounted our horses; and after crossing the fertile plain extending to the coast, and passing through the rich gardens encircling Jaffa, dismounted at the hospitable house of Asaad-el-Kayat.

I shall now endeavour, by the aid of communications received from friends at Jerusalem, to give an idea of the state of things in the city during the late exciting period.

After my departure, the position of parties camping without the walls speedily became very unpleasant, if not positively unsafe; and cannot be better depicted than in a letter from the same kind friend, to whose hospitality, on the Mount of Olives, I had so often been indebted. "You rightly conjecture," he observes, "that we are now occupying our premises on Mount Zion. We remained in our old *ruin* on Mount Olivet until both ashamed and afraid to resist the importunities of our Mussulman friends; when reasonably admonished by the nocturnal showers of stones with which some of our English friends were serenaded, we retired to our "stronghold" on the cliff of Zion; for, disorderly and dangerous as it is in the city, it is yet far more so in the country, which swarms with marauding and belligerent parties of the neighbouring Fellaheen and transjordanic Bedawin. 'Without are fightings, within are fears.' Every man now does, and that with perfect impunity too, not only 'what seemeth right in his own eyes,' but that also which is abominably wrong in the eyes of all. How different the present state of affairs from that of the palmy days of Judah's king; when there was 'neither adversary nor evil occurrent, nor complaining in our streets!' The poor Jews are truly in evil case; and though 'so long scattered, and peeled, rooted out, and trodden under foot,' in every land, they seem to bend the neck with but poor grace to the yoke of oppression in their fatherland. It taxes our own forbearance to the very utmost, to endure unresisting the taunts and threats now so freely directed against all Franks by the excited Moslem rabble.

"About forty Jews, and three or four Armenians, coming in

pilgrimage to the Holy City, the day before yesterday, were robbed of all they had near Ramleh. One of the Turkish customhouse officers was also robbed of several thousand piastres, the same day, between this city and Bethlehem. These robbers are becoming almost as daring and reckless within the city walls as beyond them; having even ventured so far to outrage Mussulman feeling as to strip the Mosque-el-Aksa of large quantities of sheet lead: but to narrate these robberies, thefts, extortions and villanies, would be as uninteresting as endless."

In view of the impending struggle with Russia, orders were sent from Constantinople to call the battalion of soldiers from Jerusalem to the seat of war,—a measure which created the greatest uneasiness among both Turks and Christians. The scene of their departure is admirably described by an eye-witness, in a letter sent to the *Times*:—"I heard the sound of drums and fifes, and great shouting and singing. I ran out of the office, and, as I expected, the soldiers were leaving Jerusalem. Such an affecting sight I think I never saw: there was scarcely a dry eye on the plain. There, outside the Jaffa Gate of Jerusalem, about 3,000 people, from the town and the villages, were congregated to wish the soldiers farewell, and success against the Russians. Here was a little crowd of peasant women and children, bewailing, with piercing shrieks, the departure of a son or husband, a brother, a father, or a bridegroom; there an assembly of Moslems, in deep grave consultation as to what would next turn up; one hoping that general war might be declared, in order to exterminate the infidels, (poor short-sighted fellow!) another hoping that peace might be made up before the departure of the soldiers; and scattered all about were solitary women and children, weeping and crying in heartrending shrieks: and this is all the effect of the mere rumour of war. Presently the soldiers arrived, *i.e.* all the entire number of regular infantry in the pashalic of Jerusalem, with the kaimacam and colonel at their head, and poor Dr. Labo following them. I stood next to Hajiz

Pasha, Governor of Jerusalem; and next to him, on the other side, stood the kadi, who, when the soldiers were drawn up in line before us, began a litany for the Sultan, in a solemn but impressive voice. At the end of every supplication, an ejaculation of 'Amen' was poured forth from about 4,000 mouths, which rent the air with their enthusiasm. When finished, each individual Moslem repeated the *Fathali*, or Moslem *Te Deum;* and the officers of the regiment each separately received the kadi's blessing, and then, taking leave of their friends, departed in mournful peace to seek for war. Now that all the soldiers have left this pashalic, the gates of the city are left to the care of special constables, who were formerly confection-sellers in the streets of the city. I can hardly imagine a number of fortified places, such as Jerusalem, Acre, Damascus, Beyrout, in a country where the differences of religious opinions are so palpable, even to the dress of the persons professing them, and all so fanatical and bigoted, left in so deplorable and unprotected a state as Syria is at the present moment. Only imagine that there is not now a single disciplined soldier in all Palestine and Syria, excepting those who are on their way to Jaffa, whence they will go to Erzeroum."

It may be well supposed that the withdrawal of the only force that could repress the turbulent spirit of the neighbouring skeihs, or enable the pasha to maintain order within the city, was viewed with the greatest apprehension, not only by the native Christians, but even by European residents. But whether it were owing to the united influence of the consuls, or to other causes, the results were far less serious than could have been expected, in a city so entirely unprotected, and split up into so many hostile parties; although too numerous outrages were committed, which the authorities had little or no power to prevent or punish.

The endless rumours that had so long been afloat, were at last cut short by the formal declaration of war by the Porte against

Russia, on which occasion a salute of twenty-one guns was fired from the citadel. "Judging," says a resident, "from preexisting excitement, I had no idea that the announcement of actual hostilities begun would be taken so coolly; but for this degree of tolerance we are doubtless indebted to Turkish notions of fatalism. I have heard some of them say it is decreed that this year the 'Nussaraneys' (or Christians) are to overcome them, but their dominion is only to last 'seven hours, or seven days, or seven years,' and then they are to enter upon a fresh career of glory and conquest, that is to eventuate in the establishment of the universal empire of Islamism, and the regeneration of the whole human family!"

By order of the pasha, the public crier announced throughout the various bazaars, that, "although war was now actually existing, they must all attend to business as usual, and continue in peace with each other." *Taib!* He told them, at the same time, that they must all pray for the Sultan; and, by way of securing the benefit of their intercessions, declared that whoever would not thus pray for the Sultan every twenty-four hours, should receive stripes—I forget how many. Thus far we are most agreeably disappointed, and have great cause for thankfulness to a kind providence, that our apprehensions of an outbreak have proved to be groundless.

The sheiks of the neighbourhood naturally took advantage of the absence of the soldiers, and the weakness of the pasha, to renew their ancient feuds. The most serious was that between Abu Ghosh, of turbulent notoriety, and Osman of Laham, a very warlike sheik from the neighbourhood of Gaza. This quarrel began in the middle of June, and continued till the middle of October. The parties drew together their respective clansmen, and assembled on the plain of Rephaim, just without the city. A pitched battle was for some days expected to come off; but the interposition of the consuls, backed by an embassy from the Pasha of Damascus, and especially by a few cannon-shot lent to Abu Ghosh by the Pasha of Jerusalem, resulted in a temporary pacification. There are still on hand several sworn wars of extermination between neighbouring villages. In the score or two of battles, or rather skirmishes, that have occurred within a few miles of the city, not more than fifty or sixty have been actually killed; but no language could well exaggerate the revolting atrocities that have been perpetrated by the "faithful."

At length, after Jerusalem had been for five weeks without a single soldier, a battalion, about a thousand strong, arrived from Aleppo; which enabled the liberal-minded pasha, who had witnessed with deep regret the commission of outrages he had no means to prevent, at length to impose order upon the belligerent sheiks. During the progress of the quarrel, the poor Bethlemites paid rather dearly for the neutrality they endeavoured to observe in the late war. Abu Ghosh, (in whose territory they reside,) summoned them to his aid, and on their refusing to participate in the war, he sent three hundred horsemen to quarter upon them, by way of commutation for military service; but they soon found the entertainment of such guests rather onerous and annoying. So they stealthily conveyed themselves and most of their effects into the convent, where they were forthwith besieged by their late guests, and many auxiliaries from the neighbouring Taamarahs; and for some days the walls around the manger of the "Prince of Peace" were enveloped in the smoke of gunpowder. At last, making a desperate *sortie*, the Christians drove the "faithful" to Beit-Jala, whence, after a few fatal shots had been exchanged, they retreated in turn, and thus ended this little military episode.

At length this dispute, which had so long kept the neighbourhood in a state of convulsion, was brought to an end in the following manner:—A few of the Syrian consular authorities, in conjunction with some of the Moslem "powers that be," organized themselves into a kind of "Peace Congress," and, acting upon the principle so pathetically urged by Miss Jeannette,

"If Kings must show their might,
Why, let them that make the quarrels
Be the only men to fight;"

recommended the bellicose chiefs to settle their disputes by single combat. This proposition, however, though eagerly embraced by one of the parties, was just as prudently declined by the other, who happened not to have so much bone, sinew, and muscle, as his more athletic antagonist. But all mediation was in vain, till the pasha took the field at the head of a strong artillery force, and razed to the ground, not only a few of their strongholds, but the entire village of Wellijeh, a few miles down the Valley of Roses. This high-handed demonstration was attended by the best effects, and the city and neighbourhood at once became perfectly quiet.

The only interruption to the peace of the city, since this time, was a fresh quarrel between the Greek and Latin monks; which, however, was not long in being settled. We may, with every reason, attribute this immunity from disturbance at such a season, to the influence of the different consulates,—and pre-eminently to that of England.

www.ingramcontent.com/pod-product-compliance
Lightning Source LLC
Chambersburg PA
CBHW021350230426
43666CB00006B/474